# BRAND METRICS

This book gathers and explains the key brand analysis tools that measure brand effectiveness and awareness along the customer journey.

Rather than considering how to build and manage a brand, *Brand Metrics* shows students the methods by which they can assess the current market position of the brand and design effective strategies for the future. Each chapter follows the same logical and accessible structure, defining each metric and its usage, presenting the calculations, showing how the data should be interpreted, offering case studies and examples, presenting recommendations and offering questions for further discussion. The metrics covered in the book correspond with the customer journey, moving through measuring brand awareness, consideration and purchase, to customer loyalty and brand advocacy, and finally an overall analysis of the brand's strength.

The book not only shows the formula for a metric and explains how it should be interpreted, but also considers what each metric really measures, how it impacts the brand's equity and how it is related to other metrics. As such it should be perfect recommended reading for advanced undergraduate and postgraduate students of Strategic Brand Management, Marketing Planning and Strategy, Marketing and Branding Metrics.

**Jacek Kall** is lecturer in marketing at WSB University, Poznan, Poland.

# BRAND METRICS

## Measuring Brand Efficacy along the Customer Journey

*Jacek Kall*

Routledge
Taylor & Francis Group
LONDON AND NEW YORK

First published 2022
by Routledge
2 Park Square, Milton Park, Abingdon, Oxon OX14 4RN

and by Routledge
605 Third Avenue, New York, NY 10158

*Routledge is an imprint of the Taylor & Francis Group, an informa business*



*British Library Cataloguing-in-Publication Data*
A catalogue record for this book is available from the British Library

*Library of Congress Cataloging-in-Publication Data*
Names: Kall, Jacek, author.
Title: Brand metrics: measuring brand efficacy along the customer journey / Jacek Kall.
Description: Abingdon, Oxon; New York, NY: Routledge, 2022. | Includes bibliographical references and index.
Identifiers: LCCN 2021012592 (print) | LCCN 2021012593 (ebook) | ISBN 9780367765033 (hardback) | ISBN 9780367765040 (paperback) | ISBN 9781003167235 (ebook)
Subjects: LCSH: Brand name products–Management. | Consumers' preferences. | Branding (Marketing)
Classification: LCC HD69.B7 K3497 2022 (print) | LCC HD69.B7 (ebook) | DDC 658.8/27–dc23
LC record available at https://lccn.loc.gov/2021012592
LC ebook record available at https://lccn.loc.gov/2021012593

ISBN: 978-0-367-76503-3 (hbk)
ISBN: 978-0-367-76504-0 (pbk)
ISBN: 978-1-003-16723-5 (ebk)

Typeset in Bembo
by Deanta Global Publishing Services, Chennai, India

# CONTENTS

# ILLUSTRATIONS

## Diagrams



## Figures



## Tables

# INTRODUCTION

Only 41 brands of Interbrand's Top 100 Best Global Brands in 2000 were still in the ranking 20 years later (Interbrand 2021). Many of the strong brands from two decades ago, such as Nokia, Yahoo or AOL, have either failed or have fallen out of customers' favour. The reality that three out of every five of the strongest global brands cannot retain their position in the ranking in just 20 years is a hard lesson of branding in the volatile 21st century.

When discussing brands, metrics certainly sound less sexy than storytelling, content and influencer marketing and many more. And unlike the above-mentioned and many other important tools in the brand-building process, metrics alone do not create a brand. It's just that they allow you to assess the current market position of a brand and help design effective strategies for the future. Brand managers in particular should become fans of numbers and metrics because in branding it is not only creativity that matters. Or rather, not just creativity based on intuition alone.

There's no agreement on who coined the phrase describing three kinds of falsehoods: 'lies, damned lies and statistics' (Department of Mathematics 2012). Obviously, one should approach the numbers behind metrics with caution, yet it is incomprehensible how many companies ignore the informational value of brand metrics. As the report conducted by the *Financial Times* and the Institute of Practitioners in Advertising (*The Board-Brand Rift* 2019) shows, half of the respondents declare the lack of metrics measuring a brand's health that are credible to senior management, and close to 40% stress the need for more understanding in their companies on how brand strength and health deliver commercial value. Accordingly, just 27% of companies report and examine brand health key performance indicators at the board level.

As with every book on metrics, this one should help the reader better understand individual metrics (of which 35 have been presented), their importance, as well as their implications for the process of brand building. However, two things make this book different.

Less emphasis has been placed on the mere calculation of metrics (although in several of the more complex cases, sample calculations are included in chapters under the section titled 'Example'), and more on their interpretation and brand-building recommendations. In each chapter, the metrics presented are defined, and formulas for calculating them are described as well as the sources of data needed. Next, the interpretation of the metric and limitations on its use are specified. Where possible, some reference values are shown, and for more complicated metrics some alternative ways of calculating them are suggested (58 formulas for 35 metrics are provided). Numerous examples of the actual values of brand metrics are covered in this book (under the section titled 'Cases' in each chapter). They come from different markets and different product categories.

The second difference is that in other textbooks, metrics are arranged according to the marketing instrument or the area they are meant to analyze. In this book, they are systematized by the stages in a customer's journey (Figure I.1). We know that each stage has different objectives, and metrics are explained in that context. They are grouped into seven chapters with the concluding chapter dealing with the holistic metrics of a brand's overall health. Some additional material explaining major concepts regarding the metrics in Chapters 1–7 is provided in the appendices.

The metrics covered in this book can be divided into two categories:

1. Metrics documenting *behaviour* (purchase), sometimes called 'hard' (Binet and Field 2007) or 'customer behaviour' (Katsikeas et al. 2016), in which buyers' preferences are *revealed*, including trial purchase, penetration rate, repeat purchase rate, brand's share of wallet, share-in-shops-handling, customer retention, sole brand users and market share.
2. Metrics analyzing *knowledge*, *perception*, *attitudes* and *intentions*, in which the preferences of buyers are *declared*, sometimes referred to as the 'customer mindset' (Katsikeas et al. 2016) or 'intermediate' (Binet and Field 2007), including assisted and spontaneous awareness, top-of-the-mind awareness, brand in top 3, brand consideration, brand purchase intention, Customer Satisfaction Index, Customer Loyalty Ratio, Net Promoter Score, Brand Advocacy Index and Brand Advocacy Ratio.

Many of the intermediate metrics react quickly and strongly, and are quite easy to link to marketing activities. Yet, 'hard' metrics should always come first as

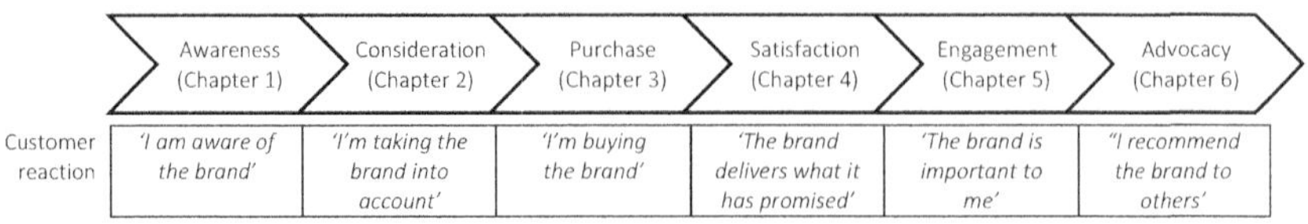


**FIGURE I.1** Stages of a customer's journey with the corresponding customer reaction.

they directly impact business performance. Therefore, when choosing a few metrics (see Epilogue) to evaluate a brand's health, priority should be given to 'customer behaviour' metrics.

The recommendation to treat hard metrics as more important and more objective is understandable. However, we should remember that there are no brand purchases if consumers are unaware of the brand. In such a case, one can buy a product with the label, but not 'the brand'. Nor can the brand have an impact on sales, if the customer is completely indifferent to it. Repeat purchases cannot be accomplished without prior satisfaction and an emotional bond with the brand. What's more, metrics that analyze customer behaviour always refer to the past, while brand awareness, brand consideration, etc., predict future purchases. The value of the 'customer mindset' metrics is therefore mainly diagnostic. They can be used as leading indicators of anticipated business success. Therefore, it would be unwise to limit the evaluation of a brand's health to hard metrics only, considering others to be of no value at all.

I express hope that in their future careers, today's marketing graduates will remember the differences between numeric and weighted distribution, between the customer retention rate and sole brand users, between market share and share of wallet, all covered in this book. And if their older colleagues, today's brand managers, better understand the conclusions that individual metrics entitle them to, and what decisions to make on their basis, my satisfaction as an author will be even greater. Understanding the link between marketing activities and brand metrics should help managers in adjusting marketing resources and activities in future branding campaigns. Metrics should be used for learning, and not just justification of previous decisions. And the more brand managers can demonstrate how their brand contributes to their company's financial outcomes, the better their relationship with the chief financial officer (CFO).

## Literature

Binet L., Field P., 2007, *Marketing in the Era of Accountability: Identifying the Marketing Practices and Metrics That Truly Increase Profitability*, World Advertising Research Center, Henley-on-Thames.

Cassidy, F., 2019, *The Board-Brand Rift: How Business Leaders Have Stopped Building Brands*, *Financial Times* + IPA, London.

Department of Mathematics, 2012, *Lies, Damned Lies and Statistics*, University of York, www.york. ac.uk/depts/maths/histstat/lies.htm [access: 3.01.2021].

Interbrand, 2021, *Desire: In the Decade of Possibility – Best Global Brands 2021*, Interbrand c_space.

Katsikeas C.S., Morgan N.A., Leoindou L.C., Hult G.T.M., 2016, Assessing Performance Outcomes in Marketing, *Journal of Marketing*, 80, pp. 1–20, doi: 10.1509/jm.15.0287.

# 1

# MEASURING BRAND AWARENESS

**Learning objectives:**

After reading this chapter you should

- understand what brand awareness is and why it is necessary for building a strong brand;
- be able to discuss the role of categorization in understanding awareness measurement;
- be familiar with three awareness metrics: aided awareness, spontaneous awareness and top-of-the-mind awareness;
- understand the concepts of 'brand salience' and 'brand dominance';
- recognize the limitations of awareness metrics.

We are at the beginning of the customer's journey. Customers need to be aware that a brand exists that might solve their problems or deliver promised rewards. It is the brand owner's first responsibility to make the brand 'visible' in places where its target audience might be looking for solutions to their problems. And this does not necessarily mean that a brand must be active on mass media.

## 1.1 Awareness explained

There is no doubt that if we think of a brand, its strength and its influence on the decision-making process and user satisfaction, then the brand must be *known* to the buyer. If a consumer standing in front of a store shelf is considering buying a no-name product, it is probably a result of the need for variety-seeking (e.g. 'I have never eaten those sweets, I have never heard of them, but I will gladly try them, just out of curiosity because the package looks so funny'), which is

DOI: 10.4324/9781003167235-1

accompanied by a limited risk (low probability of dissatisfaction with consumption, and in the case of dissatisfaction, a small financial loss). However, such situations of buying unknown brands just out of curiosity are rare. Our reptile brain (see Appendix 1) definitely feels safer when choosing known objects, and not completely unfamiliar ones. Aaker (2011) claims that consumers prefer what is familiar to them in every aspect of their lives. And if we think of building a strong brand, we need to understand that consumers cannot love a brand of which they have barely heard (Steenkamp 2017). It is not surprising then, that there is a strong correlation between brand awareness and brand trial (see Section 3.2.1), as observed by Nielsen Market Research Agency among others (Watts 2020).

Now, let's return to the purchase decision-making process. Consumers start their shopping by *choosing a product category*, the purchase of which will provide them with rewards or allow them to avoid problems. But only then will they choose the brand. It's hard to imagine that desire comes first, 'I have to buy something from Bosch, Samsung, …', and only then is the decision made to choose the product from those brands. Even for such a strong brand as Apple, the hierarchy of decisions is predictable: product category (tablets, smartphones) and then the brand and model. In seldom cases (those exceptions might be the purchase of clothes, but also such a mundane category as bakeries), the decision sequence might be the opposite: we first decide which fashion store or bakery to enter, and only when we are inside will we choose specific products: slouchy or slim fit jeans? baguette or bread?

If that is so, we first need to understand how the consumer groups the offerings of different companies operating within a specific category (a process called 'categorization'), which will help us in measuring awareness.

### 1.1.1 Categorization

**Definition**: *The process of grouping objects into categories based on the perceived similarities between them is called* ***categorization****.*

Categorization makes it easier to deal with a lot of information reaching our brain. Psychologists Stasiuk and Maison (2014) explain that for human beings, seeing their surroundings through the lens of categories is natural and categorization is crucial in the process of learning about and understanding the world around us. With regard to products, De Plessis (2011) states that consumers will inevitably classify all new brands in terms of existing product categories. When shopping, by assigning a brand to a specific category, the need to seek further information is reduced (Aaker 2011). Because I have decided I need a tablet and not 'any device functioning thanks to the operating system and software, with the help of which you can do various tasks and enjoy games or films' (this condition is met by a smartphone, laptop and desktop computer, and to some extent also a smart TV and a few other devices), further decisions (which brand, which model) can be taken much faster.

When encountering a new brand, consumers usually use the following heuristics (Aaker 2011):

1. Assigning a brand to a category based on matched (usually) visible attributes. Each category/subcategory has a specific set of ideal attributes, and a new brand can be assessed on a 'zero-one' basis. Either a brand is included in the category or not, on the basis of whether it meets all conditions. Or a brand's assignment to a category depends on the degree of matching its attributes to the ideal. Sometimes, it is enough to meet the most important criteria, but in other cases, all criteria must be met, at least to a satisfactory level.
2. Assigning a brand to a new category as its standard, its exemplar. One brand might become a category standard (Prius, iPad, Tesla), when it was the category's innovator or early leader and the brand that had a dominant influence on its development, while at the same time impacting customers' expectations. Another case is when listing the ideal attributes is not simple, but one brand manages to impose an image of an exemplar in some respects (safe car = Volvo).

It should be noted that categorization is a dynamic process, so categories' boundaries may change depending on the consumption or shopping context (Pogorzelski 2015). The brand is not assigned to a specific category once and for all. Brand managers would like to divide the market into categories at their own discretion, of course, but such conventional categorizations, used to analyze the market, do not necessarily correspond to categories in the minds of buyers.

The evaluation and perception of categories (what I think about tablets or, more specifically, what I think about tablets based on Android) will have a relatively *greater* impact on the decision-making process than the evaluation and perception of a particular brand within the category/subcategory (what I think about the Huawei MediaPad compared with my opinions about Samsung's Galaxy). This is due to our natural tendency to *stereotype*, i.e. reduce the importance of the differences between objects (brands), while exaggerating the similarities between them. It should be clear that the role of a brand owner is to counteract stereotyping by differentiating the brand in the customer's mind.

The initial assignment of a brand (e.g. Santander or Diesel) to a specific category (banks and jeans, respectively) or a subcategory (retail bank/designer jeans) determines, in the long term, those brands' perception (what are banks/jeans like in general) and what is expected from them. In other words, I will evaluate Santander/Diesel from the perspective of my expectations towards banks/jeans. This shows why categorization is so important in the context of branding.

When purchasing a specific category, the buyer relies to some extent on his/her memory and on brands that have been coded into it. The lower the level of the purchase involvement of a category, because the product is less important for the buyer, and its purchase is associated with a relatively lower risk, the weaker the motivation for the buyer to actively search for information outside his/her memory (Stasiuk Maison 2014). The fact that within a category the consumer recalls only a few brands does not mean that he/she has consciously rejected all the others. Usually, those other brands are simply not noticed by the consumer, maybe due to their low availability in stores or the lack of communication activities on their side or poor visibility on the store shelves. Therefore, regardless of how good the product of a given brand objectively is, its sales success largely depends on the ease of recalling the brand from memory in the context of a specific decision-making situation. If the shopping context is different (because of whom a product is purchased for: 'for myself' vs. 'as a gift for a loved one', or because of the place where the product is consumed: beer in a pub vs. beer in front of the TV at home), other brands can be recalled from memory.

Time has come to define what awareness is and how it can manifest itself.

### *1.1.2 Brand awareness*

**Definition**: Brand awareness is the ability of a buyer who is trying to satisfy his/her needs to recognize (after being exposed to brand elements: its packaging, name, logo, etc., on a store shelf, a company's website, in a public space) or to recall (in the same situations, but without seeing/hearing brand elements, the customer can recall its name or characteristic packaging elements from his/her memory) brand elements to the extent which makes an informed choice possible.

Consider the case of buying a specific drug at a pharmacy. Brand awareness will manifest itself in any of the following situations:

(1) asking the pharmacist about a specific drug by name, no matter whether the name is pronounced correctly or not, as long as the pharmacist understands precisely which drug is in question;
(2) asking the pharmacist about a drug for a specific ailment, whose brand name a patient cannot recall, yet remembers well the specific design of the packaging and can describe it to the extent that the drug can be accurately identified;
(3) asking the pharmacist about the medicine for a specific ailment and after hearing a few names suggested by the pharmacist, a patient can indicate unmistakably the one sought;
(4) asking the pharmacist about the medicine for a specific ailment and after being shown a few packages, the patient indicates the one sought;
(5) noticing the medicine for a given ailment on a shelf and indicating the packaging to the pharmacist.

In each of these situations, it is the brand that is used to make an informed choice about a specific drug.

How well brand elements are encoded in a buyer's memory depends, among others, on the frequency of purchase of a given category of drugs; on the date of the last purchase; how severe the condition is for the patient; and whether the patient is buying the medicine for himself/herself or another person. However, regardless of whether the brand of the drug was properly recalled, or it had to be somehow prompted (by showing the packaging or mentioning the name), the choice of the drug was conscious, not accidental ('please, give me any of them') or determined by the low price ('please give me the cheapest one'), nor was it the pharmacist's suggestion ('what would you personally take') or the product's popularity ('please give me what most people buy').

As to the awareness metrics, aided awareness measures brand recognition, and spontaneous and top-of-the-mind awareness measure brand recall.

## 1.2 Aided brand awareness

### Metric definition

*Aided/prompted brand awareness* is the percentage of product category buyers who can recognize the brand, specifically its name, logotype or packaging, when shown on a list, on a shelf or on a computer screen.

### Metric calculation

$$\begin{aligned}&\text{Aided brand awareness}\\&\quad = 100 \star \text{number of consumers declaring they know/have heard}\\&\qquad \text{about the brand (even if faintly)} : \text{number of category buyers}\end{aligned} \tag{1.1}$$

### Metric interpretation

Of all the metrics at this stage of a customer's journey, aided awareness always achieves the highest values, because of the smallest effort that the brain must make to confirm having heard about the brand. What's more, aided awareness will sometimes be high due to the respondent's incorrect conviction that he/she recognizes the brand, although in fact its name, logotype or packaging resembles a different brand (sometimes even in a different product category). It is therefore recommended to add to the list of brands a non-existing one (with the name and maybe even a logo or packaging, created for the needs of the survey), to check how much aided brand awareness in a particular case can be overestimated. Experience proves that fake brands are usually recognized by a few, sometimes even 12 (one has heard of cases of so-called *spurious* awareness exceeding 20) percentage points of category buyers surveyed. Therefore, that metric's score for an examined brand should refer not only to the category leader but also to the aided awareness of non-existing brands. For example, if we obtained the following values for aided brand awareness: leader 65%, brand X 16% and non-existing brand 12%, it is difficult to interpret such a situation positively ('after all it is not bad, every sixth buyer of the category has heard about our brand'). While the high level of aided awareness cannot be explicitly interpreted as evidence of the market success of a brand, widespread ignorance among buyers of a given category certainly signals problems for the brand owner.

For a buyer, the very fact that a brand is 'somehow known to him/her', he/she has 'heard something about it' can be interpreted as evidence that for some reason it must be a better option than a completely unknown brand. The classic research of Zajonc from the late 1960s proves that repeated exposure to a new stimulus (regardless of how attractive it is objectively) causes people to start to like it more. Even the ordinary packaging of an ordinary brand looks nicer at a second look than it does when seen for the first time. Lee (1994) explains this with the heuristics of accessibility. The repetition of exposure to a stimulus causes its faster recognition, and recognized stimuli are usually more liked (East et al. 2008).

Aided awareness is therefore important, even for goods rarely purchased, with a high level of risk involved. In such a situation, it is obvious that before purchasing, the buyer will actively engage in searching for information by asking friends, by consulting online forums, by reading reviews either online or in the press, or by asking sellers about available offerings within a given category. However, an information search is limited to brands known to the buyer. It is impossible to consult a brand website or ask friends' opinions on brand XYZ of a tablet or coffee machine if you are not aware that such a brand exists!

Of course, online tools supporting the purchase of a product (e.g. price comparison websites) make it easy to learn about brands whose existence we have not previously been aware of. The only question is whether such additional alternatives that are found at the last minute are welcomed by the prospective buyer. Let's imagine that we want to buy a laptop. In the most popular e-stores you can buy some 20 brands and thousands of different models of laptops. Suppose that from my own experience (as a user) I know four brands, and I know another three brands from the opinions of my friends and websites dedicated to that category. Isn't it sensible to filter an e-store's offer to those seven brands? What is the point of including in the comparisons, brands I have never heard of before and only learned about their existence by accident through consulting a website? In fact, research commissioned by Google (2019) on consumers in Central and Eastern Europe indicates that when purchasing consumer electronics, as much as 90% of consumers get their information online, of whom the vast majority (72%) use a search engine (39% visit the websites of manufacturers and 30% use YouTube). The chances of looking for information about a brand that you are unaware of are practically nil.

## Cases

(1) *Polish Kompania Piwowarska*[1] *(from 2017 part of Asahi Breweries Europe Group) has, for many years, been the leader or vice-leader of the Polish beer market, offering 11 national and international brands (2021). Two among them are Tyskie Gronie and Zubr (European bison, in Polish). Their aided brand awareness scores for the succeeding quarters of 2018 and 2019 are presented in Table 1.1.*

**TABLE 1.1** Prompted brand awareness of selected brands of beer in Poland (2018–2019)

| | *Q1 2018* | *Q2 2018* | *Q3 2018* | *Q4 2018* | *Q1 2019* | *Q2 2019* | *Q3 2019* | *Q4 2019* |
|---|---|---|---|---|---|---|---|---|
| Zubr | 92 | 90 | 87 | 86 | 89 | 89 | 89 | 89 |
| Tyskie Gronie | 89 | 87 | 85 | 86 | 86 | 87 | 87 | 87 |

Source: Company data.

(2) *In 2015, the aided brand awareness of* The Economist *magazine among the US population was 44% (Burnett 2016).*
(3) *In 2020, Dekoral paint (a brand with over 20 years of history in Poland, owned by PPG Industries) had an aided awareness of 81% (Dekoral 2020).*

**Metric limitations**

Lately, there has been some controversy over whether marketing investments to train consumers' minds to easily recognize brand names are enough to build a strong brand. Analyzing a vast amount of data, Kantar consultancy (2020) has found that not so much brand recognition, but a brand's ability to conjure positive, instant meaning and a feeling of the right choice are more important in achieving high levels of sales because they lead to a more automatic and less reflective choice by consumers.

What's more, in some cases, customers might recall the brand because it had been involved in a scandal or offensive or unethical activities. That kind of recognition cannot have a positive impact on a brand's strength.

## 1.3 Spontaneous brand awareness

**Metric definition**

*Spontaneous/unaided brand awareness* measures brand recall and determines what percentage of category buyers can retrieve the brand elements (usually name) from memory.

**Metric calculation**

Spontaneous brand awareness

$$= 100 \star \text{number of consumers recalling the brand from memory} : \text{number of category buyers} \tag{1.2}$$

**Metric interpretation**

The level of spontaneous awareness for every brand is significantly lower than aided awareness. The differences between the two usually range from 30 to even 60 percentage points. The more aided awareness (brand recognition) differs from spontaneous awareness (brand recall), the stronger the possibility of some image problems. The consumer, for some reason, is not urged to remember the brand, although he/she knows well that it exists. This may suggest disappointment in the past, a long time since last contact with the brand or a significant change in the tastes and preferences of the consumer.

Generally, achieving a high level of spontaneous awareness, especially in fast-moving consumer goods (FMCG), is difficult. This is because of the limited memory resources allocated to brands in categories that are not very important to the consumer, especially if the majority of the competing brands appear to be very similar. Why, then, remember several dozen brands of mineral water if recalling three or four of them seems enough to do everyday shopping? On the other hand (again, especially in the case of FMCG), there is a *strong correlation between a brand's spontaneous awareness and its market share*. The reason is quite banal. It is more convenient/faster for the consumer to buy a brand strongly established in memory than to deliberate which one to choose at every shopping trip.

## Cases

(1) *Spontaneous brand awareness of the British Automobile Association (AA), the largest provider of breakdown services in the UK, dropped from around 97% in 2005 to 77% at the end of 2012. The major culprit was a reduction in brand-building communication. The awareness rose again to 94% in 2017, after an emotional TV campaign (Sussman 2018).*

(2) *Spontaneous awareness of the German car brand Audi in the UK rose from 22% in 1999 to 49% in 2014 (Lion Gwin 2020).*

(3) *Spontaneous awareness scores for two Polish brands of beer (Tyskie Gronie, Zubr), for the succeeding quarters of 2018 and 2019 are presented in Table 1.2.*

(4) *Direct Line is a British brand that, in 1985, transformed the insurance industry by eliminating the middleman, which resulted in cost savings for customers. In the time period of 32 months (January 2013–September 2015), the spontaneous brand awareness for Direct Line in the case of car insurance varied between 34% and 47% and in the case of home insurance between 31% and 39%. Peaks and troughs (a maximum drop of 11 percentage points within two months) strongly correlated with the brand's TV spending (Bratton et al. 2016).*

The case of Direct Line strongly supports Sharp's notion about the real nature of brand awareness. Sharp (2017) suggests that brand awareness as such is *probabilistic*,

**TABLE 1.2** Spontaneous brand awareness of selected brands of beer in Poland (2018–2019)

| | *Q1 2018* | *Q2 2018* | *Q3 2018* | *Q4 2018* | *Q1 2019* | *Q2 2019* | *Q3 2019* | *Q4 2019* |
|---|---|---|---|---|---|---|---|---|
| Tyskie Gronie | 70 | 68 | 69 | 70 | 69 | 68 | 69 | 71 |
| Zubr | 47 | 49 | 47 | 46 | 50 | 47 | 46 | 47 |

Source: Company data.

which means that the same brand in certain contexts (determined, among others, by the mood of the consumer, earlier mental processes or the time of day, week or year) may be more easily recalled or with difficulty. The ease of recalling a brand from memory mainly depends on how fresh and how extensive (number and quality) the network of neural connections is, of which a brand is a component. Running an advertising campaign just before a survey increases brand awareness for a while. The metric drops by a few percentage points soon after an advertising campaign ends.

On the other hand, a very large increase in brand awareness seems to be a good predictor of the economic success of a brand, at least in the case of fast-moving consumer goods. The Institute of Practitioners in Advertising (IPA) databank, which is a collection of case studies prepared for the UK's IPA Effectiveness Awards,[2] shows that in 80% of very successful (in business terms) communication campaigns, very large awareness improvements were registered (Binet Field 2007).

**Metric limitations**

When asking about brands known to a respondent, we usually restrict the question to a product category, the nature of need or shopping occasions. When analyzing spontaneous awareness, it is good to know the exact phrasing of the question, because addressing a specific occasion (whiskey brands consumed at meetings with friends) compared to a broad definition of the product category (whiskey? high-alcohol spirits?) will result in different values of awareness for the same brand.

## 1.4 Top-of-the-mind awareness

**Metric definition**

*Top-of-the-mind awareness* determines the percentage of buyers of the product category who, when asked about brands known to them, mention the brand in the first place.

**Metric calculation**

$$\text{Top-of-the-mind awareness} = 100 \star \text{number of consumers mentioning the brand as the first within a given category} : \text{number of category buyers} \quad (1.3)$$

**Metric interpretation**

For every brand, top-of-the-mind awareness is significantly lower than spontaneous awareness, just as spontaneous awareness is much lower than aided awareness. You need to remember that 'top-of-the-mind' of all brands in a category is, by definition, limited to 100%, which is not the case for spontaneous or aided awareness.

Analyses indicate that brands with large market shares differ much more in top-of-the-mind values than small brands. All 'small' brands have very low levels of top-of-the-mind awareness. At the same time, large brands do not vary much in spontaneous awareness (they all have relatively high levels), but strongly differ from small brands (Romaniuk et al. 2004).

### Case

*The relations between prompted, spontaneous and top-of-the-mind awareness scores for two Polish brands of beer are presented in Table 1.3.*

Many brands, although generally known (aided awareness), are not mentioned by anyone, as the first brand in a category. As you can guess, mentioning the first brand in a category is a sign of the unique relationship between the consumer and the brand. Either the consumer is buying only this brand or would like to (aspire) buy it, or he/she considers it the best or largest in the category. Therefore, a high value for top-of-the-mind awareness can be considered as evidence not only of being deeply rooted in customers' memory but also of having built some emotional bond with them.

### Cases

(1) *In 2017, the top 5 women's cosmetic brands in South Korea, with the highest top-of-the-mind awareness scores were: Amore Pacific Sulwhasoo (10.9%), Amore Pacific Hera (7.4%), Amore Pacific (3.5%), Amore Pacific Iope (2.9%) and LG Ohui (2.1%) (Statista 2019).*

(2) *Top-of-the-mind awareness scores for two brands of beer (Tyskie Gronie, Zubr) for the succeeding quarters of 2018 and 2019 are presented in Table 1.4.*

### Metric limitations

A higher top-of-the-mind score for a brand does not necessarily mean that it is used by a larger number of customers, nor that it is more popular among them than a brand with a lower top-of-the-mind score (see Table 1.5).

**TABLE 1.3** Awareness metrics for Tyskie and Zubr (2019)

| *Metric* | *Tyskie Gronie* | *Zubr* |
|---|---|---|
| Top-of-the-mind | 19 | 7 |
| Spontaneous brand awareness | 69 | 47 |
| Prompted brand awareness | 87 | 89 |

Source: Company data.

**TABLE 1.4** Top-of-the-mind brand awareness of selected brands of beer in Poland (2018–2019)

| | *Q1 2018* | *Q2 2018* | *Q3 2018* | *Q4 2018* | *Q1 2019* | *Q2 2019* | *Q3 2019* | *Q4 2019* |
|---|---|---|---|---|---|---|---|---|
| Tyskie Gronie | 22 | 19 | 18 | 20 | 19 | 18 | 20 | 20 |
| Zubr | 5 | 6 | 7 | 6 | 7 | 7 | 6 | 7 |

Source: Company data.

**TABLE 1.5** Top-of-the-mind awareness vs. yearly penetration rate vs. most often used brand for three brands of beer in Poland (2019)

| | *Top-of-the-mind* | *Penetration* | *Most often used brand* |
|---|---|---|---|
| Tyskie Gronie | 19 | 39 | 9 |
| Lech Premium | 14 | 37 | 7 |
| Zubr | 7 | 37 | 9 |

Source: Company data.

**Case**

*Top-of-the-mind awareness and most often used brand scores for three brands of beer are presented in Table 1.5. Although Zubr has just half of the top-of-the-mind score for Lech Premium, their yearly penetration rates (see Section 3.2.2) are exactly the same, and Zubr has even a little higher score on 'most often used brand'.*

### *1.4.1 Brand salience and brand dominance*

In the case of FMCG, an increase in spontaneous brand awareness is achieved at the expense of other brands. The barrier is the consumer's unwillingness to remember many brands in a mundane product category, so the improvement in recall of one brand must result from forgetting another. In such a case, we are dealing with so-called *brand salience*, which manifests itself in the lack of motivation to remember other brands, such as when a given brand is well known to the consumer and most likely meets his/her needs at the maximum level. This applies, for example, to brand XYZ shown in Table 1.6.

When asked about brands known in a given category, recalling brand XYZ in the first place eliminates the need to remember other brands so they obtain spontaneous awareness levels from 15% to 25%. In turn, for each of the competitors, mentioning them in the first place does not mean that buyers do not remember about brand XYZ. Apparently, brand XYZ is in some way unique, or is perceived as a leader of the category, which urges consumers to remember it.

In an extreme situation, when only one brand is commonly known in a given category, such a case is defined as *brand dominance*. Thirty years ago, this was the situation on the kitchen salt market in Poland. The only brand obtaining

**TABLE 1.6** Brand salience – hypothetical example

| *Other brands recalled spontaneously* | *First brand mentioned (top-of-the-mind awareness)* | | | |
|---|---|---|---|---|
| | *XYZ (%)* | *BCD (%)* | *LMN (%)* | *OPR (%)* |
| XYZ | – | 75 | 65 | 70 |
| BCD | 25 | – | 30 | 20 |
| LMN | 15 | 20 | – | 20 |
| OPR | 20 | 15 | 20 | – |

(in each region of the country) significant levels of spontaneous awareness was Wieliczka (where famous salt mines can be visited). Marketing textbooks often give the example of Bacardi as the only widely known representative of the rum category. We shall note that many really strong brands (e.g. Ferrari in the sports car market) have not built such dominance. Of course, the question 'what is a Ferrari?' produces the correct answer that it is a sports car, but the question 'what brands of sports cars do you know?' usually produces a few brands, not just one.

When a brand dominates a category, it becomes its only representative, a kind of 'standard', and sometimes even a colloquial term for the product (such as Kleenex for disposable tissues or Adidas as a common term for sneakers in Poland).

## Recommendations for brand managers

1. Levels of aided awareness comparable with rivals should be taken for granted, if a brand is supposed to successfully achieve the next stage in the customer's journey. If the relative aided brand awareness is very low, this is a strong signal that a brand is barely known. In any case, aided awareness below 20% is proof that the brand is totally unknown to customers. If a brand is relatively new to the market, a change in communication (channels, content) is needed or a higher budget is required. In the case of brands with a long history and high prompted awareness scores, this metric should not change much (as can be seen in Table 1.1), so a long-term decline in aided awareness is a signal of problems, but not only with brand communication.
2. In the case of FMCG brands, a high level of spontaneous awareness is usually proof of a relatively high market share. High relative spontaneous awareness in the case of big-ticket items might be a signal that a brand is at least taken into consideration by many customers. But beware, those brands that have had their glory days (e.g. Nokia in the case of smartphones) might still be easily recalled by many customers. A high level of spontaneous awareness is absolutely desirable but not enough to call the brand 'strong'. Thus, consulting the 'brand in the top 3' or the 'brand consideration' metric is strongly recommended.
3. On the other hand, low spontaneous awareness accompanied by high aided awareness is nearly always proof of image problems. An in-depth, qualitative attitude measurement (see Chapter 2) is a must in such a case.
4. Only the strongest brands have a top-of-the-mind awareness higher than their competitors. They are either market leaders or brands that are perceived as market leaders, or most innovative, or most liked. Most probably, brands with the highest levels of top-of-the-mind awareness have also the 'best' image of all brands in the category, meaning the associations built in customers' minds are most favourable, or they have more favourable (and less negative) associations than their competitors.

## Questions

1. Why is brand awareness important for the market success of a brand?
2. For which products/services is awareness relatively more important?

3. What is the difference between spontaneous and aided awareness? How does it impact the interpretation of those metrics?
4. What is the difference between top-of-the-mind and spontaneous awareness? How does it impact the interpretation of those metrics?
5. What is so-called spurious awareness?
6. What does brand salience mean?
7. What does brand dominance mean? How can we diagnose such a situation?

## Notes

1 All the information in this chapter regarding that case has been delivered by the Consumer Insights Team of Kompania Piwowarska.

2 At the time of writing Binet and Field's (2007) book, the database contained 880 case studies.

## Literature


Aaker D.A., 2011, *Brand Relevance – Making Competitors Irrelevant*, Jossey-Bass, San Francisco.

Binet L., Field P., 2007, *Marketing in the Era of Accountability: Identifying the Marketing Practices and Metrics That Truly Increase Profitability*, World Advertising Research Center, Henley-on-Thames.

Bratton C., Constantine A., Pietersma N., 2016, Direct Line: We Solve Problems, in: *Advertising Works 23: Proving the Payback on Marketing Investment*, ed. B. Angear, Institute of Practitioners in Advertising + WARC, London, pp. 139–163.

Burnett D., 2016, The Economist: Raising Eyebrows and Subscriptions, in: *Advertising Works 23: Proving the Payback on Marketing Investment*, ed. B. Angear, Institute of Practitioners in Advertising + WARC, London, pp. 351–375.

Dekoral, 2020, *Czolowe Marki Konsumenckie i biznesowe w Polsce*, Superbrands Polska, Warszawa, pp. 38–39.

Du Plessis E., 2011, *The Branded Mind, What Neuroscience Really Tells Us about the Puzzle of the Brain and the Brand*, Kogan Page, London.

East R., Wright M., Vanhuele M., 2008, *Consumer Behaviour: Applications in Marketing*, SAGE, Los Angeles.

Google, 2019, *Think with Google: Journey of a Smart Shopper – Consumer Electronics in CEE*, December.

Kantar, 2020, *BrandZ 100 Most Valuable Global Brands*.

Lee, A.Y., 1994, The mere exposure effect: is it a mere case of misattribution, in: *Advances in Consumer Research*, ed. C.T. Allen, D.R. John, No. 21, pp. 270–275.

Lion W., Gwin Th., 2020, Audi: The Value of 'Vorsprung Durch Technik' over Four Decades, in: *Advertising Works 25: Proving the Payback on Marketing Investment*, ed. S. Unerman, Institute of Practitioners in Advertising + WARC by Ascential, London, pp. 87–117.

Pogorzelski J., 2015, *Marka na Cztery Sposoby*, Wolters Kluwer, Warszawa.

Romaniuk J., Sharp B., Paech S., Driesener C., 2004, Brand and Advertising Awareness: A Replication and Extension of a Known Empirical Generalisation, *Australasian Marketing Journal*, 12(3), pp. 70–80, doi: 10.1016/S1441-3582(04)70107-X.

Stasiuk K., Maison D., 2014, *Psychologia konsumenta*, PWN, Warszawa.

Statista, 2019, *Top-of-Mind Women's Cosmetics Brands South Korea 2017*, 24 July, www.statista.com/statistics/782702/south-korea-women-cosmetics-brand-top-of-mind-awareness/ [access: 28.12.2020].

Steenkamp J.-B., 2017, *Global Brand Strategy: World-wise Marketing in the Age of Branding*, Palgrave Macmillan, London.

Sussman T., 2018, The AA: From Spark-Plugs to Singalongs, in: *Advertising Works 24: Proving the Payback on Marketing Investment*, ed. N. Godber, Institute of Practitioners in Advertising + WARC, London, pp. 305–348.

Watts G., 2020, *Innovating in the Digital Era: The Evolving Role of Digital Media on New Product Launches*, Nielsen, www.nielsen.com/us/en/insights/article/2020/innovating-in-the-digital-era-the-evolving-role-of-digital-media-on-new-productlaunches/ [access: 30.12.2020].

# 2

# MEASURING BRAND CONSIDERATION

**Learning objectives:**

After reading this chapter you should

- recognize the limitations of measuring attitudes;
- understand why there is no perfect 'attitude metric';
- be familiar with four metrics based on customers' declarations: brand consideration, brand in the top 3, brand preference and brand purchase intention.

## 2.1 Why no attitude metrics?

In the next stage of the customer's journey, when the brand is no longer unknown, a potential buyer might begin a closer inspection. The buyer checks whether the brand may solve his/her problems or deliver the desired rewards. The consumer is now open to arguments regarding the brand. If the consumer finds the decision to be complex because of the product's price and expected importance, he/she might actively seek information about the brand, wishing to know its advantages over its competitors. Or, in the case of low-involvement purchases, the consumer may be passively exposed to a brand's arguments presented on social media or in the mass media, on the packaging and in the stores. The role of brand communication is to provide arguments/opinions that will cast the brand in a more favourable light, and may even encourage close inspection of it (testing). In a word, a brand owner wants to influence a positive attitude towards the brand.

DOI: 10.4324/9781003167235-2

### 2.1.1 What is brand attitude?

We might view a brand as a conglomerate of a customer's experiences with it, tagged emotionally with a 'plus' or a 'minus' sign (see Appendix 1). When a brand has been providing us with pleasure, mere exposure to its packaging is enough to feel that sensation. Research shows that the reward for the brain, which is a flood of dopamine, appears *before* performing a specific action (using the brand) and not as a result of it (Magrini 2017). When, on the other hand, a brand is associated with dissatisfaction (disappointment), then just thinking about it prompts you to discard it from the set of brands taken into account when shopping. Those brand associations that result from personal experiences are retrieved from the memory more rapidly and have a stronger impact on individual behaviour because of the way they were imprinted (East et al. 2008). Unfortunately, despite the phenomenal career of neuromarketing research,[1] we do not have access to brand associations in customers' minds (Satel and Lilienfeld 2015).

How do marketers deal with those limitations? By creating a construct defined as consumers' attitude towards a brand.

**Definition**: ***Brand attitudes*** *are the result of a positive or a negative predisposition towards a brand (the affective component), based on beliefs (a cognitive component) about it, which in turn affects the tendency for specific brand-related behaviour (conative component). Humans learn attitudes or acquire them through personal experiences, exchanging opinions with others regarding their memories of brand experiences, obtaining information from different sources or on the basis of an inference. Thus, not only former sensory experiences related to the brand, past emotions and feelings, but also logical arguments made in connection with the brand purchase, as well as attempts to rationalize it, contribute to shaping brand attitude (van Praet 2012).*

### 2.1.2 Is brand attitude really that important?

Sharp's (2017) point of view regarding attributing an important role to brand attitudes in the shopping decision-making process is full of reservations. For the past few decades, psychologists (contrary to many marketers) have tended to downplay the role of attitudes in explaining human behaviour. Although consumers buy thousands of brands throughout their lives, most of those purchases do not arouse any strong emotions. Additionally, in the overwhelming majority of cases, they buy not so much a 'brand' as a marketing construct, but above all a product that is a reliable/proven solution to a particular problem. It might be hard to admit for marketers, but the key motive for buying various products is not the irresistible need to enter the world of the brand, nor the obligation arising from a close relationship built with it, nor the fascination with a story told by the brand owner. Customers purchase products/services in order to achieve various sensory or mental rewards (ice cream in a favourite flavour or an engaging book), or to avoid sensory or mental punishments (painkillers or travel insurance). The choice of a particular brand is quite often just a way to simplify shopping, by customarily purchasing the same brand in the context of a given need/situation. This can be compared to the behaviour of our ancestors tens of thousands of years ago roaming the plains of Africa, who preferred well-known plants and fruits over those they had not tried before. Those choices were safe and promised pleasure instead of pain (Van Praet 2012). Or maybe the explanation for preferring known over unknown brands might be the natural tendency discovered by Kahneman (2011) and Tversky to prefer safe alternatives in a situation of choice that could result in potential gain (discovery of a new brand)? Nevertheless, apart from a few exceptions, most brands evoke just lukewarm emotions. And it's hard to expect that it might be otherwise. We have so many really exciting things to do in our lives that another jar of mayonnaise or a roll of kitchen paper is unlikely to excite us. Indeed, even the purchase of durable goods with a high price tag will usually cause only a fleeting thrill (Harari 2015).

At the same time, emotions are present in many decisions, even regarding product categories that strongly engage us in the decision-making process (Calne 2010). In situations where a decision is complex and we don't have all the information needed, we have a tendency to rely both on reason and emotion. Gut feeling is the common human experience of making a quick and easy decision, which makes us feel good, although we would have problems explaining it using rational arguments. It seems that such fast responses to external stimuli, based on past biological, personal and cultural experiences, are clearly helpful in everyday life. Of course, when we have enough time to work things out, we would rather rely on reason. The problem is that, in many cases, we do not have that time.

Returning to brand attitudes, Sharp (2017) claims that they reflect past behaviour rather than determine future choices. We like brands that we have trialled before and therefore it is the change in shopping behaviour that modifies attitudes, and not (as the marketing textbooks used to claim) the other way around. This manifests itself in the fact that brands with higher penetration (bought by a larger number of buyers) usually have better ratings in the affective dimension (liking). Consumers unaware of the brand or having little knowledge about it cannot say they like it very much. Therefore, brand attitude reflects the existing relationship to the brand: the more often a brand is bought by consumers, the more they like it (Ehrenberg 1998).

Secondly, according to Sharp (2017), brand attitudes are supposed to be probabilistic. In surveys repeated on the same sample, only half of the respondents show a stable attitude towards the brand (research by Ehrenberg's team). Usually, surveys are carried out not on the same sample but on samples of other respondents; therefore, popular brands get approximately the same percentage of positive responses, although from different respondents, giving the impression of stable brand attitudes. Attitudes are largely based on a respondent's memory, which is not, as we know, perfect. As Sharp explains, respondents tend to declare that they like one brand best and then next time, declare the same about another brand because both of them are in their repertoire of brands (see also Chapter 5) purchased, yet neither of them evokes any passionate feelings. Ehrenberg (1998) draws similar conclusions, suggesting that if there are differences in brand attitudes within a category, they relate more to each brand's specific attributes or applications, rather than to the affective component. What's more, the mood in which the consumer finds himself/herself can have a significant impact on changing the brand's evaluation (Stasiuk and Maison 2014).

Thirdly, one can have doubts whether in each product category buyers code into their brains an extensive system of neural connections with brands' associations. Does every brand of table salt, spices or toilet paper really have such an extensive engram (system of neuronal connections) in the minds of customers? Sharp (2017) warns not to take respondents' declarations regarding their brand attitudes at face value. Consumers sometimes do not know what they feel about a brand until they have been asked in a survey. This is the reason why there is only a 50% chance of respondents giving the same answer when asked again about their brand attitude. Other researchers partly blame the very questionnaire used to measure attitudes, claiming that it may force respondents to come up with a brand attitude even in product categories that they do not consider thoroughly, so in fact they know very little about the brands offered (Priluck and Till 2010).

Last but not least, there is no proof that improving brand image automatically leads to better sales. As Binet and Field's (2007) analysis of dozens of advertising campaigns in the UK proves, over half of those campaigns that were highly effective in business terms recorded small or no improvement in brand image. Image is hard to change, and campaigns that try to do so are not terribly successful.

### *2.1.3 Measuring brand attitudes*

Attitudes are usually the subject of a separate research project because they are complex and require many research methods, as they cover different areas. In a very broad sense, attitude research should include (as proposed by Keller 2013): judgements regarding a brand's quality, credibility, superiority; feelings (warmth, fun, excitement, security, social approval, self-respect) that a brand evokes; a brand's imagery (user image, occasion image and brand personality, among others); and opinions regarding the brand's performance (reliability, durability, efficiency, style, design, price). In effect, attitude research is usually more complicated, time-consuming and costly than researching brand awareness, loyalty and satisfaction (Baalbaki and Guzmán 2016). Each dimension of attitudes is analyzed using an extensive set of scales or qualitative techniques, and effects do not take the form of numbers, but verbal accounts. Obviously, the interpretation is less clear-cut than in the case of the numerical metrics described in this book, and to some extent depends on the experience of the researcher. It is not only the techniques used in measuring attitudes that can influence the diagnosis, but also the subjectivity of the researcher, even just by emphasizing in the final report the selected opinions about the brand that emerged during interviews, if they correspond with the views of the researcher.

Needless to say, *brands with high market share and penetration perform better in attitude research*. An important question arises whether extensive attitude research is needed in a situation where all relevant metrics regarding brand, namely: awareness (especially top-of-the-mind), sales (high and increasing penetration; high and increasing share of wallet; high and increasing market share), satisfaction and loyalty, and availability (high/growing weighted distribution; high/growing share-in-shops-handling) irrevocably prove that a brand has a strong market position. In such a case, attitude research seems to be (1) of no particular value (since no alarming symptoms are present) and (2) potentially confusing. It is possible that in one of the focus group interviews there might be one critical opinion of an extremely demanding user, which might distort the generally positive brand image.

Of course, attitude research might prove useful in some cases, but it is worth bearing in mind four restrictions:

1. Even without research it is known that large brands (high market share and penetration) must have a generally positive image, and smaller brands (small market share and low penetration) may have a good reputation, but only with a small group of buyers (usually positive opinions will be correlated with a brand's share of wallet; see Section 5.5). Attitude towards the brand depends on how often it was bought in the past, and what is its share of requirements. Buyers with a brand's share of wallet exceeding 50% have in their minds more associations regarding it than buyers with a share of wallet below 20% (Romaniuk and Nenycz-Thiel 2013). It is hard to expect that before the first purchase of the brand, consumers will have an extensive set of associations regarding it. Indeed, research proves that current brand users are four or five times more prone to spontaneous associations with a brand than non-users (Romaniuk et al. 2012). If we add Sharp's (2017) remarks cited earlier (the repetition of a survey on the same sample will reveal slightly different attitudes towards a brand than previously declared), we will fully understand on what thin ice we walk.
2. Different research agencies use different techniques, and are particularly sensitive to the words used (let's take adjectives only: 'modern' in one research is not the same as 'contemporary', 'up to date' or 'current' in others), which make results not fully comparable. What is more, a significant part of attitude research is descriptive in nature, which makes it difficult to compare the results over time and across categories. When analyzing two research reports regarding two different brands, it is not easy to say univocally which has a more positive attitude ('better image'). For this reason, it would be wiser to prepare one questionnaire with an agreed list of attributes, occasions of consumption or personality traits and not to change it in subsequent rounds of the surveys.

3. Research on attitudes is usually qualitative rather than quantitative, which results in the high susceptibility of decision makers to a single, controversial statement that appears in the research report. The best image can easily be ruined by one vivid and critical opinion of one participant in the group interview, quoted in the final report.
4. There is a growing belief among researchers that consumers are not always aware of the sources of their attitudes (some of them are out of their control) and, moreover, that some attitudes are implicit. Consumers might be unaware of some emotions and beliefs regarding a brand, and those create their latent attitude which may strongly influence purchase decisions. As a consequence, there is a move away from measuring attitudes based on introspection in favour of indirect measurement based on autonomous reactions, e.g. analyzing reaction time (Stasiuk and Maison 2014). That kind of research is obviously beyond the scope of this book.

It is understandable that the adoption of any metrics for such complex matters as consumer opinions and attitudes always looks a bit simplified. The four metrics suggested below *do not provide the full picture* of how a brand is perceived, but they can help to capture alarming signals, which should lead to the use of more sophisticated and sensitive procedures described above.

## 2.2 Brand consideration, brand in top 3

Brand consideration is a reliable metric of brand health because it is closely linked to actual behaviour (Binet and Field 2007). In two-thirds of hundreds of communication campaigns analyzed by Ebiquity and Gain Theory, brand consideration had the strongest link to base sales. A one percentage point increase in consideration usually drove a 0.5–1.5 percentage increase in base sales (Profit Ability: The Business Case for Advertising 2018).

### Metric definition

*Brand consideration* is the percentage of consumers who would consider purchasing a brand, usually by answering a question on a 5-point scale (the so-called 'consideration scale'): 'I would definitely consider buying a brand'; 'I would rather consider buying a brand'; 'Don't know/hard to say...'; 'I would rather not consider buying a brand...'; 'I would never consider buying a brand...'.

### Metric calculation

We might simply take the percentage of 'I would definitely consider buying a brand...' or calculate the brand purchase consideration (as below) and compare it with rivals:

$$\begin{aligned}\text{Brand purchase consideration} = {} & 5 \star \text{ percentage of definitely consider} \\ & + 4 \star \text{ percentage of rather consider} \\ & + 3 \star \text{ percentage of hard to say} \\ & + 2 \star \text{ percentage of rather not consider} \\ & + 1 \star \text{ percentage of would never consider}\end{aligned} \tag{2.1}$$

Some research agencies use their proprietary tools. For example, YouGov offers a service named BrandIndex where brand consideration is measured by a question: 'When you are in the market next to purchase items in this particular category, from which of the following brands would you consider purchasing?'.

**Metric interpretation**

If, in comparison to competitors, the average value of a brand is closer to 5 ('I would definitely consider buying'), or the percentage of 'would definitely consider' is higher than the brand's competitors, this proves the brand's high level of appeal to potential buyers.

**Cases**

(2) *In February 2018, 'brand purchase consideration' among US customers, in the case of selected car brands, as measured by YouGov BrandIndex was as follows: Hyundai – 16.1%; Jeep – 15.1%; Kia – 13.1% ('Cloverfield' Effect 2018).*
(3) *In 2019, 'brand consideration' in the case of Audi was 68% among the UK's prestige audience (those who already owned a prestige car); in the case of BMW it was 63%; and in the case of Mercedes 56% (Lion and Gwin 2020).*
(4) *DFS has been supplying sofas to British customers for about half a century and was the leading retailer of living room furniture in 2017. Its brand consideration index in 2017 was 42% as measured by YouGov (Ross 2018).*
(5) *AA's emotional spots aired in 2017 increased brand purchase consideration from 52% to 58% (Sussman 2018).*

Contrary to classical models of the decision-making process, which assumed that a consumer moving closer to a final purchase decision was supposed to narrow the number of brands considered (the so-called 'consideration set'), a large research project carried out by McKinsey indicates that today this set rather *broadens* as a result of the process of information search and the exchange of opinions (Court et al. 2009). For example, according to Nielsen (2018), as the purchase gets nearer, the number of car brands under consideration doubles. This may be due to the fact that the set of attributes used to decide whether to include a brand in a consideration set, after exchanging information with other product users (e.g. on internet forums), might be expanded to encompass new, not previously considered brands (Dawar 2013).

If a brand is among the top 3 brands in a particular category, it has a much higher chance of market success.

**Metric definition**

*Brand in top 3* determines the percentage of category buyers who declare they would include a brand in a set of three brands most likely to be considered in the decision-making process.

**Metric interpretation**

If the examined brand is among the *top 3 brands* in a category (is among three brands with the highest ratings), we believe that this indicates an overall positive attitude towards it.

**Cases**

(2) *In the UK retail market, in 2014, the top 3 brands in terms of 'quality' were Marks & Spencer, Waitrose and Sainsbury's, while in terms of 'value': Aldi, Lidl and ASDA (Gregory and Parnum 2020).*

(3) *Audi managed to top the ranking of the premium cars market in the UK in the dimension 'make cars with intelligent technology', with 42% of respondents agreeing that Audi is associated with that attribute (in the case of two major competitors their ratings were 41% and 38%) (Lion 2018).*

## 2.3 Brand preference

Another metric suggesting a positive attitude is brand preference.

**Metric definition**

*Brand preference* is the percentage of category buyers declaring their preference for a given brand, if the price and the availability of all brands in a category were the same.

**Metric calculation**

In a survey, we ask category buyers which brands in a category they prefer, under the assumption that price and availability are the same for all.

**Metric interpretation**

If the percentage of respondents who prefer a given brand, when compared to competitors, is higher, then its attitude and overall attractiveness are better. In the case of cheaper brands, it tests their appeal when compared with more expensive competitors. In other words, it helps to separate the impact on a customer's decision of a brand, from the impact of price and availability.

**Case**

*Direct Line, mentioned in Chapter 1, has been the leader of the UK's direct insurance market for several years since its market launch, achieving around 10% of the car insurance market in 1997. In the mid-2000s, price comparison websites started stealing market share from direct insurers and, as a result, from autumn 2012 to summer 2014, the percentage of consumers considering Direct Line fell from 25.3% to 21.4%. In summer 2014, Direct Line's brand preference, in the case of car insurance, was at 11.3% and in the case of home insurance it was 9.6%. A year later, following a new advertising campaign ('The Fixer'), the preference for Direct Line in the case of cars increased to 15% and for home to 14%. It is worth noting that second-rank brands in both cases had a 12% preference rate (Bratton et al. 2016).*

## 2.4 Brand purchase intention

When it comes to asking about intentions to buy, it is necessary to include three elements: (1) the purpose of the purchase (for personal use or for someone else, and if so for whom?); (2) the context of the purchase (in which store? online? offline?); and (3) the context of use situation (in what situation? which season of the year, day of the week, time of the day?). Without specifying 'for whom, where and for what', the respondent cannot be expected to provide an unequivocal answer.

**Metric definition**

*Brand purchase intention* determines the percentage of category buyers who declare they are going to purchase a particular brand on their next shopping trip.

**Metric calculation**

In response to the question 'How likely is it that the next time when you buy... (what? for whom? in which shop? in what context of use?), you will choose brand X?', respondents choose from an 11-point scale proposed by Juster (East et al. 2008): from 0 'no chance, almost no chance', through 5 'fairly good possibility' to 10 'certain, practically certain'.

$$\text{Brand purchase intention} = \text{sum of products}\left(\text{percentage} * \text{value}\right) \tag{2.2}$$

**Metric interpretation**

If, in comparison to competitors, brand purchase intention is closer to 10 ('certain, practically certain'), this proves the high level of a brand's appeal to the potential buyer.

Sometimes, a respondent is asked just to choose which brand in a category he/she will buy next time.

**Case**

*According to a 2019 survey of Australian consumers about car brands they intended to purchase within the next four years, 16.8% of respondents mentioned Toyota, 8.7% said they intended to buy a Mazda and 7.6% declared it would be a Hyundai (Statista 2019).*

**Metric limitations**

For years, researchers have been asking consumers about their intentions to buy a brand, treating it as a kind of test of all the activities in the area of so-called acquisition marketing. If purchase intentions had increased after a marketing campaign, it was evaluated as effective. The problem with analyzing the intention to purchase a brand is twofold.

First of all, often the question about intentions has an incorrect form (see remarks above).

Secondly, the results of such questions are sometimes misinterpreted. The fact that 20% of category buyers declare they will purchase brand X for personal use next time they are in their regular shop, cannot be considered as a guarantee of achieving a certain level of sales. Research shows that purchase intentions are not always fulfilled. Especially in the case of high-value items, under the influence of various circumstances (such as a change in family or professional situation) affecting disposable income, intended purchases may be postponed or the decision about the product (e.g. smartphone not a tablet) and/or brand being purchased (e.g. Xiaomi not Oppo) might change (Gupta and Zeithaml 2006). Sharp (2017) claims that purchase intentions paradoxically are correlated with *past rather than future* brand choices, and that intentions can be proof of the effectiveness of communication activities in the case of goods with a high unit value, but not the basis for sales forecasts. Here, Sharp cites research on American consumers regarding car purchase intentions within the following 12 months. It turned out that among those planning to buy a car, in the following year the purchase was actually made by 40%, while among those not planning to buy a car, 7% actually bought one. As a result, most cars (over 60%) were bought by consumers who had not planned to buy a car a year before, when the survey was carried out.

Why are purchase intentions weak in predictive capacity? In the case of most regularly purchased product categories, purchase intentions are decided just before the moment of purchase, as they do not require saving significant sums of money. For this reason, when asked about future purchases, respondents usually indicate the brand they are currently buying, assuming rationally that choosing the current brand is more probable/easier/safer.

Therefore, new brands entering the market with low penetration rates have no chance of performing well in questions on purchase intentions. Analyzing intentions to purchase, one might infer that the market situation will never change; that brands that sell well will continue to dominate, and brands with small shares have no chance of success.

### Recommendations for brand managers

In view of the above, the following approach seems most appropriate:

1. In the case of actual brand buyers, until there are some signals from the analysis of selected metrics (sales, satisfaction, loyalty), for your own peace of mind you might systematically analyze brand consideration and/or brand purchase intention, especially in the case of brands of big-ticket items.

2. When some alarming signals arise from the above-mentioned metrics (much lower than competitors' or decreasing), or you want to learn about the brand attitudes of consumers who have not experienced the brand, it is wise to conduct syndicated research preferably with a reputable research agency that has developed and tested for years their own methodology of attitude research. It should be remembered that the buyer's attitude towards the brand is always relative. A customer evaluates a brand as more or less (than competitors) capable of satisfying his/her needs and wants. Therefore, when measuring attitude it is necessary to take it into consideration ('X is the best of the available brands on the market', 'is one of the best brands' and so on up to 'the worst of the brands available on the market').
3. Only when research reveals 'scratches' on a brand's image, in-depth research covering all the areas described above (brand's performance; its credibility and superiority over others; the perceptions of a typical user and usage context, personality; emotions that the brand evokes) should be commissioned.

### Questions

1. Why is attitude research more complicated than measuring brand awareness?
2. How can we prove that the overall attitude towards the brand is positive?
3. When asking about brand purchase intentions, what elements must be included?
4. How can the Juster scale be used in measuring brand purchase intentions?
5. Can we take declarations regarding brand purchase intentions at face value?
6. Why are purchase intentions weak in predictive capacity?

## Notes

1 Stasiuk and Maison (2014) compared our fascination with neuromarketing research to that of subliminal advertising several decades ago, which resulted in uncritical faith in their findings.

## Literature

Baalbaki S., Guzmán F., 2016, Consumer-Based Brand Equity, in: *The Routledge Companion to Contemporary Brand Management*, ed. F. Dall'Olmo Riley, J. Singh, Ch. Blankson, Routledge, London, pp. 32–47.

Binet L., Field P., 2007, *Marketing in the Era of Accountability: Identifying the Marketing Practices and Metrics that Truly Increase Profitability*, World Advertising Research Center, Henley-on-Thames.

Bratton C., Constantine A., Pietersma N., 2016, Direct Line: We Solve Problems, in: *Advertising Works 23: Proving the Payback on Marketing Investment*, ed. B. Angear, Institute of Practitioners in Advertising + WARC, London, pp. 139–164.

Calne D., 2010, *Within Reason: Rationality and Human Behavior*, Vintage, New York.

'Cloverfield' Effect: Netflix Scores the Super Bowl's Biggest Lift in Purchase Consideration", 2018, *Advertising Age*, 7 February.

Court D., Elzinga D., Mulder S., Vetvik O.J., 2009, The Consumer Decision Journey, *Mc Kinsey Quarterly*, 3, www.mckinseyquarterly.com/The_consumer_decision_journey _2373 [access: 20.12.2020].

Dawar N., 2013, *Tilt: Shifting Your Strategy From Products to Customers*, Harvard Business Review Press, Boston.

East R., Wright M., Vanhuele M., 2008, *Consumer Behaviour: Applications in Marketing*, SAGE, Los Angeles.

Ehrenberg A.S.C., 1998, Repetitive Advertising and the Consumer, in: *How Advertising Works: The Role of Research*, ed. J.Ph. Jones, SAGE, Thousand Oaks, pp. 63–81.

Gregory S., Parnum J., 2020, From Running Shops to Serving Customers: The Tesco Turnaround Story, in: *Advertising Works 25: Proving the Payback on Marketing Investment*, ed. S. Unerman, Institute of Practitioners in Advertising + WARC by Ascential, London, pp. 47–86.

Gupta S., Zeithaml V., 2006, Customer Metrics and Their Impact on Financial Performance, *Marketing Science*, 25(6), pp. 718–739, doi: 10.1287/mksc.1060.0221.

Harari Y.N., 2015, *Sapiens – A Brief History of Humankind*, Harper Collins Publishers, New York.

Hutchins, N., House, B., 2018, *The Nielsen Auto Marketing Report*, The Nielsen Company (US).

Kahneman D., 2011, *Thinking Fast and Slow*, Farrar, Straus and Giroux, New York.

Keller K.L., 2013, *Strategic Brand Management: Building, Measuring, and Managing Brand Equity. Global Edition*, Pearson, Harlow.

Lion W., 2018, Audi UK: Beauty and Brains: How We Supercharged the Audi Premium 2015–2018, in: *Advertising Works 24: Proving the Payback on Marketing Investment*, ed. N. Godber, Institute of Practitioners in Advertising + WARC, London, pp. 45–82.

Lion W., Gwin Th., 2020, Audi: The Value of 'Vorsprung Durch Technik' over Four Decades, in: *Advertising Works 25: Proving the Payback on Marketing Investment*, ed. S. Unerman, Institute of Practitioners in Advertising + WARC by Ascential, London, pp. 87–118.

Magrini M., 2017, *Cervello. Manuale dell'utente. Guida semplificata alla macchina più complessa del mundo*, Giunti Editore, Firenze-Milano.

Priluck R., Till B.D., 2010, Comparing a Customer-Based Brand Equity Scale with the Implicit Association Test in Examining Consumer Responses to Brands, *Brand Management*, 17(6), pp. 413–428.

*Profit Ability: The Business Case for Advertising*, 2018, Ebiquity+Gain Theory Special Report.

Romaniuk J., Bogomolova S., Dall' Olmo Riley F., 2012, Brand Image and Brand Usage: Is a Forty-Year-Old Empirical Generalization Still Useful?, *Journal of Advertising Research*, June, pp. 243–251, doi: 10.2501/JAR-52-2-243-251.

Romaniuk J., Nenycz-Thiel M., 2013, Behavioral Brand Loyalty and Consumer Brand Associations, *Journal of Business Research*, 66, pp. 67–72, doi: 10.1016/j.jbusres.2011.07.024.

Ross A., 2018, Turning DFS from a Value Brand into a Brand That People Value, in: *Advertising Works 24: Proving the Payback on Marketing Investment*, ed. N. Godber, Institute of Practitioners in Advertising + WARC, London, pp. 113–156.

Satel S., Lilienfeld S.O., 2015, *Brainwashed: The Seductive Appeal of Mindless Neuroscience*, Basic Books, New York.

Sharp B., 2017, *Marketing: Theory, Evidence, Practice*, 2nd Edition, Oxford University Press, Sydney.

Stasiuk K., Maison D., 2014, *Psychologia konsumenta*, PWN, Warszawa.

Statista, 2019, *New Vehicle Buying Plans by Brand in Australia 2019*, 12 November, www.statista.communications in statistics/1068027/australia-breakdown-intention-to-buy-a-new-vehicle-by-brand/ [access: 30.12.2020].

Sussman T., 2018, The AA: From Spark-Plugs to Singalongs, in: *Advertising Works 24: Proving the Payback on Marketing Investment*, ed. N. Godber, Institute of Practitioners in Advertising + WARC, London, pp. 305–348.

Van Praet D., 2012, *Unconscious Branding: How Neuroscience Can Empower (And Inspire) Marketing*, Palgrave Macmillan, New York.

# 3

# MEASURING BRAND PURCHASES

**Learning objectives:**

After reading this chapter you should

- understand why metrics covering brand availability are important in explaining sales of a brand;
- be able to critically evaluate the effectiveness of a brand's availability using numeric and weighted distribution;
- be familiar with five metrics explaining brand sales: numeric distribution, weighted distribution, share-in-shops-handling, trial rate and penetration rate;
- have a clear understanding of the role of the penetration rate in evaluating a brand's market position.

The final decision to purchase a brand manifests to the brand owner as sales. There are a few metrics that might be helpful in analyzing brand purchases. They can be divided into those related to final users and those related to intermediaries (retailers). The simple truth is that if we expect retail sales to grow, a brand must be available in stores. So, let us start with the retailers' perspective.

## 3.1 Retailers' perspective on brand sales

This may seem surprising especially to people with little market experience, but among all the marketing mix elements, distribution has the strongest impact on the sales of a new brand (Singh and Wright 2016). After analyzing five years of weekly data across 25 categories and 70 brands sold in the four largest chains in France, Ataman et al. (2010) found that in the long run, distribution (brand availability) has a more than five times larger relative impact on a brand's sales

DOI: 10.4324/9781003167235-3

than advertising. After analyzing seven years of four-week brand metrics, plus the sales and marketing actions of 61 brands in four product categories, Srinivasan et al. (2008) have come to the conclusion that the impact of distribution on brand awareness, brand consideration and brand liking is at least 11 times larger than that of advertising.

In the case of fast-moving consumer goods (FMCG), the ease and convenience of finding a brand in many stores selling a given product category and in stores where the product is sold in large quantities so that consumers perceive them as places where you shop for a particular category is a prerequisite for a brand's market success. A brand's availability could be due to the fact that it is available almost everywhere (it is always within reach, 'at hand', like the proverbial Coca-Cola), or that the consumer is well aware of the places where the brand can be purchased without much effort. Of course, the dynamic development of e-commerce can give the false impression that access to a brand is no longer a problem, because you can most probably find it in one of the thousands of e-stores. On the other hand, it is difficult to expect that the online purchase of product categories such as food will dominate, even in the foreseeable future. Until recently, only 3% of food sales in the United States were online purchases (Bain 2019), and it will take some time to clarify whether the Covid-19 pandemic will change that picture. BCG (2020) forecasts that by 2022, the e-commerce share of food sales will settle at about 6%–8%. The US Department of Commerce estimates that in the third quarter of 2020, e-commerce was responsible for 14.3% of total retail sales in the United States (Quarterly Retail E-Commerce Sales 3rd Quarter 2020). If this is so, an analysis of the numeric and weighted distribution can provide valuable tips on how to improve the physical availability of a brand, or explain the reasons for unsatisfactory levels of sales.

### *3.1.1 Numeric distribution*

**Metric definition**

*Numeric distribution* is the percentage of stores selling a given product category in which an analyzed brand is available.

**Metric calculation**

$$\text{Numeric distribution} = 100 * \text{number of stores selling a brand} : \text{number of stores selling a product category} \quad (3.1)$$

The total number of stores of a given trade should be easily available from official statistics or AC Nielsen audits. As to the number of stores selling a brand, estimates of either the brand's sales reps or wholesalers carrying the brand can be used. The brand owner should make some reasonable assumption as to how many stock-keeping units (SKUs) of a particular brand should be available in each store to count it as 'selling the brand' in the numerator (this remark applies to brands offering many variants, e.g. flavours and scents).

### Metric interpretation

The higher the metric's value the better, but only to a certain level. It is hard to expect huge sales success if the brand is available in, let's say, 5% of stores selling a category. In such a case, a consumer who does not know where the brand is available must visit, on average, 20 stores to find 1 store with the brand on the shelf. It seems obvious that having customers' convenience in mind, a brand should have a much higher numeric distribution.

On the other hand, increasing a brand's availability by reaching more and more stores is associated with an increase in the costs of logistics,[1] which is a real challenge in countries with fragmented distribution.[2] Increasing the numeric distribution from 85% to 90% might have a negligible impact on the convenience of shopping, yet result in reaching additional numbers (sometimes hundreds) of wholesalers and retailers, which have to be supplied.

### Case

*Eden Creamery is a California-based ice-cream manufacturer, established in 2011. They sell under the brand name Halo Top Creamery, and have developed ice cream lower in carbohydrates and refined sugars, having millennials in mind. Building availability from scratch, at retailers like Whole Foods and Sprouts (that specialize in natural foods), Halo later expanded into traditional grocery and mass channels. Their numeric distribution increased from 3% to 11% in 2016, and to more than 70% in 2017, with an average of 10 product varieties available in each store (Edelstein et al. 2018).*

### Metric limitations

In the numeric distribution, every point of sale is treated with equal importance, no matter how big it is, or how high the turnover of a given category it generates. If we take a shopper who does not know in which stores you can buy a specific product, then he/she most probably visits them on a random basis (e.g. starting from the closest one). The negative consequences of low numeric distribution can be observed here. It may happen that, although the shopper had already visited a dozen stores of a given trade (e.g. carrying foodstuffs), he/she had yet to come across the desired brand. This might be because the category is not sufficiently popular for the majority of stores to carry it (e.g. glazed balsamic vinegar of Modena). Of course, such situations are rare. Based on many years of shopping experience, consumers accumulate in their memory knowledge of what can be purchased where, and in the case of the product mentioned above, a shopper would probably go to a large hypermarket or delicatessen, rather than a small local grocery store. This brings us to an important truth: points of sale are not equal in terms of importance to shoppers and their purchase of a specific category. Therefore, perhaps even more important metric analyzing the availability of a brand is the weighted distribution, which takes into account each store's sales potential.

### 3.1.2 Weighted distribution

**Metric definition**

*Weighted distribution* (also known as 'product category volume' [PCV] distribution) indicates what proportion of sales of a given category is generated by stores that stock the brand. In other words, it indicates the proportion of the market to which a brand has access.

**Metric calculation**

$$\text{Weighted distribution} = 100 * \text{sales}\left(\text{volume / value}\right) \text{ of category in stores selling the brand} : \text{sales}\left(\text{volume/ value}\right) \text{ of category in all stores} \quad (3.2)$$

Weighted distribution can also be calculated from the transformation of Formula 7.3:

$$\text{Weighted distribution} = \text{Brand's market share} : \text{share-in-shops-handling the brand} \quad (3.3)$$

**Alternative way to calculate weighted distribution**

It is quite likely that a manager wishing to calculate a weighted distribution does not have precise data on category sales in stores where a brand is available (data on total retail sales are usually available in industry reports or other secondary sources). You can then estimate the weighted distribution provided that you have as reliable as possible (which means based on as many points of sale as possible) the category sales statistics of a typical store carrying the brand and a typical store not carrying it (Table 3.1).

**TABLE 3.1** Estimation of weighted distribution of brand X (hypothetical case)

| | *Percentage of stores (2) (%)* | *Estimated sales (value or volume) of a category per store (3)* | *Product (2 × 3) (4)* | *Weighted distribution (5)* |
|---|---|---|---|---|
| Stores offering brand X | 40* | 35 | 1,400 | 1400/2300 = **60.9** |
| Stores without brand X | 60 | 15 | 900 | |
| | | Total | 2,300 | |

* Numeric distribution.

### Case

*In 2015, L'Oréal's flagship foundation offered in the UK was True Match (fifth brand in terms of market share). The brand was mainly available (85% of brand sales) in Boots and Superdrug, and its weighted distribution was just 21%. At that time, the value market share of True Match was 6.0%. The leader of the market at that time had a 6.8% value market share and a 51% weighted distribution. In 2017, the market share of True Match had increased to 9.7% (no. 2 had only 7.3%), and the weighted distribution had increased to 28% (Ellis et al. 2018).*

### Metric interpretation

A high level of weighted distribution means that a brand is available in 'more important' stores – those responsible for a considerable part of category sales. In the example above, stores having the brand on their shelves register more than double (35/15 = 2.3) category sales compared with stores not offering the brand.

If the numeric distribution of brand X is, say, 50%, while the weighted distribution is, say, 66%, this means that brand X is available in half of all stores offering the product, yet those stores generate two-thirds of total category sales. In other words, the brand is available in 'more important' stores as they generate above average sales (in this case one-third higher than the average store; this can be calculated by dividing the weighted distribution by the numeric distribution).

In Western markets characterized by a much higher concentration of retail trade, especially in the case of frequently purchased goods, four or five retail chains usually generate 60%–70% of total sales.[3] And the research indicates that if a new brand introduced to the market gains the acceptance of buyers, within *eight months* it reaches *70% weighted distribution* (Jones and Slater 2003), which usually means that every major retail chain is carrying that brand. Later, it becomes impossible to achieve equally spectacular increases in weighted distribution.

In countries with a fragmented retail market,[4] even if FMCG brands were available in every hypermarket and supermarket and discount chain operating there (which is pretty unrealistic), they would still achieve a maximum weighted distribution level of just 50%–60%.

In so far as increasing the numeric distribution does not make sense in every case (after achieving a certain level of numeric distribution, one always reaches new stores which are less and less important from the perspective of sales potential, and costs increase proportionately), then the manager should always take care to improve the availability of the brand in 'more important' stores. Brand availability should be increased up to the moment when an additional percentage point of numeric distribution gets at least one extra percentage point of weighted distribution. Figure 3.1 presents the general recommendations regarding both metrics.

### Example

The Polish Organization of Oil Industry and Trade estimates that there are approximately 7,800 gas stations in Poland. Let's calculate the numeric distribution of a brand's product offered only through this distribution channel (gas stations), assuming that the brand is available at 60% of Orlen stations (their total

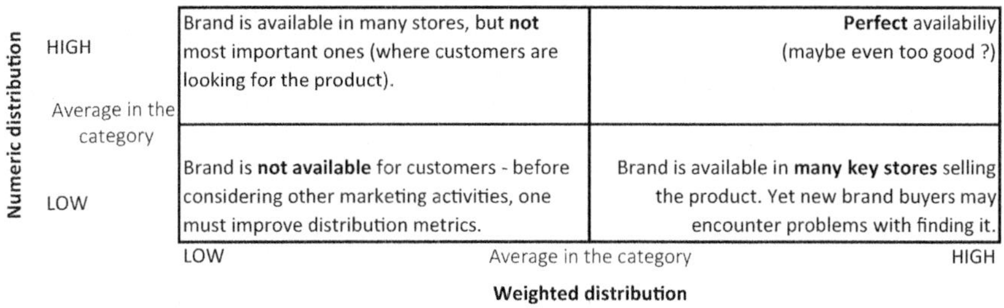


**FIGURE 3.1** How to evaluate distribution metrics?

number is 1,770) and at all Lotos stations (500 in total; Wiadomosci Handlowe 2019). The numeric distribution is easy to calculate: (0.6 ★ 1,770 + 500)/7,800 = 0.2. The availability at the gas stations of those two companies ensures the brand's numeric distribution at 20%. In other words, the brand is available at every fifth point of sale. This indicates limited availability for the customer. On average, the customer would have to visit five petrol stations randomly selected to have a chance of buying the brand in one of them.

But assessing brand availability should not only be based on the number of points of sale. Small, networked gas stations, neither in terms of product assortment offered nor the number of buyers, do not compare to those of the largest operators. Let's say that we have sales statistics for a given product (see Table 3.2).

If we assume that the brand is available in typical, average (in terms of sales of a given product) Orlen and Lotos stations, its weighted distribution is calculated as follows: 0.6 ★ 35 + 8 = 29%. Therefore, the brand in question is available at points of sale responsible for 29% of the category sales. If we refer this to numeric distribution, we can conclude that the brand is available at stations selling 45% more of the product, compared to the average for all points of sale (29/20 = 1.45). This proves that gas stations that have been selected have higher sales potential. Of course, many of those attractive points of sale still do not have a given brand in their offering (40% of Orlen stations and all foreign stations); however, in general, it can be stated that the average station in which the brand is offered now sells much more (63%) of a given product than the average station where the product is not available (29 : 20/71 : 80 = 1.63).[5]

**TABLE 3.2** Hypothetical sales data of a brand sold exclusively at petrol stations

| *Petrol stations* | *Hypothetical structure of product sales (%)* | *Share in total number of gas stations (real data) (%)* |
|---|---|---|
| Orlen | 35 | 23 |
| Lotos | 8 | 6 |
| Foreign chains | 40 | 18 |
| Other (local, independent) | 17 | 53 |

If the sales force were to improve the availability at Orlen stations (so that the brand would be available at each of them) and reach one-fifth of the chain stations belonging to foreign operators, then the availability metrics (especially the weighted distribution) would improve significantly (again, assuming that the stations where the brand will be offered are typical, i.e. average in terms of sales of the product):

Numeric distribution = 23 + 6 + 0.2 ★ 18 = 32.6%
Weighted distribution = 35 + 8 + 0.2 ★ 40 = 51%

So, the brand would now be available in nearly one-third of all petrol stations, which are responsible for over half of category sales. Petrol stations where the brand is available sell 56% more of the category than the average (51/32.6 = 1.56), which proves that a new distribution strategy is quite reasonable. At the same time, it can be stated that the average station in which the brand is offered sells much more (more than twice!) of a given product than gas stations in which the brand is not available (51 : 32.6/49 : 67.4 = 2.15).

And finally, one more interesting conclusion. The hypothetical sales strategy adopted here (all Orlen and Lotos stations and every fifth belonging to foreign chains) is more sensible from the perspective of not only brand availability for customers but also sales efficiency than the alternative of reaching (let's say) two-thirds of smaller, independent petrol stations, even if the numeric distribution would be much better in the latter case. Table 3.3 shows a comparison of the metrics in both options.

At first glance, it may seem that being available at 35.3% of points of sale (Option 2) is better than at only 32.6% (Option 1). But this simple comparison of the percentage of points of sale offering the brand ignores where customers most often shop for the product. Admittedly, in the second option, the availability measured by the numeric distribution is better, but at the same time points of sale in this option realize almost five times[6] lower sales of the product than in the first option! In the first option, we reach points of sale selling 115% more of the product than points of sale not offering the brand; in the second, there are indeed more stations with the brand on their shelves, but the average of these stations sells 77% less of the product than those where the brand is not available! The distribution

**TABLE 3.3** Comparison of two alternatives of brand availability at petrol stations

| | *Option 1: All Orlen and Lotos stations plus one-fifth of foreign chain stations (%)* | *Option 2: Two-thirds of smaller, independent local petrol stations (%)* |
|---|---|---|
| Numeric distribution | 32.6 | 35.3 |
| Weighted distribution | 51 | 11.3 |
| Product sales at stations offering the brand compared to those where brand is unavailable | 115 higher | 77 lower |

in the first option is therefore much more effective, because we reach just a few operators (therefore we have lower logistics costs, and less negotiation is needed), and each point of sale where the brand is offered has greater sales potential. In the second option, we will probably negotiate better price deals (at the opposite side of the table are business owners with weaker negotiating power), but trade talks need to be conducted with an incomparably larger number of intermediaries supplying gas stations, and then we have to deliver our brand to much higher numbers of stations, which has an impact with significantly higher costs for logistics and sales. What's more, we will reach many gas stations where product sales are quite small. And even if exclusive sales deals or preferential exposure conditions could be negotiated and our brand's share-in-shops-handling (see Section 3.1.3) in the second option would be three times higher than in the first option (let's say, 90% vs. 30%), the accessible market share is still 50% higher in the first option, because we have access to a larger part of the market (Table 3.4).

**Metric limitations**

It makes no sense to calculate numeric or weighted distribution in the case of brands of clothing, jewellery, cars and other products if the brand builds its availability on a network of its own stores. In such cases, the assessment of the physical availability of a brand should be based on two questions: comparing the number of own stores to competitors[7] and estimating what percentage of customers is provided with convenient access to the brand (for example, what share of category buyers live within a radius of a one-hour drive from stores of a particular fashion brand).

Indeed, one should not underestimate the importance of metrics related to brand availability, which not only determine the customer's comfort in purchasing the brand but are also related to costs and directly affect the potential market share of the brand.

### *3.1.3 Brand's share-in-shops-handling*

**Metric definition**

*Share-in-shops-handling* (SISH) is a specific case of market share, as long as the market is understood as category sales realized by stores offering an examined brand.

**TABLE 3.4** Hypothetical market shares in different availability options

| *Assumption* | *Option 1: All Orlen and Lotos stations plus one-fifth of foreign chain stations (%)* | *Option 2: Two-thirds of smaller, independent local petrol stations (%)* |
|---|---|---|
| Brand will achieve hypothetical level of share-in-shops-handling, of … | 30 | 90 |
| Market share | **15.3** | **10.2** |

### Metric calculation

$$\text{Share-in-shops-handling} = 100 \star \text{brand sales}\left(\text{volume/value}\right) \text{ in stores selling the brand} : \text{category sales}\left(\text{volume/value}\right) \text{ in stores selling the brand} \quad (3.4)$$

If it is not possible to calculate it on the basis of data provided by intermediaries, you can try to calculate the SISH transforming formula 7.3 as follows:

$$\text{Share-in-shops-handling} = 100 \star \text{brand's market share} : \text{brand's weighted distribution} \quad (3.5)$$

### Alternative way to calculate SISH

Knowing the average brand turnover[8] for every retail chain where a brand is available, plus the average number of brand packages standing on their shelves and the category sales at each retail chain, one can try to calculate the SISH for that chain as follows:

$$\text{Share-in-shops-handling}\left(\text{in a given chain}\right) = 100 \star \text{brand turnover} \star \text{number of brand packages on the shelves} : \text{category sales in a given chain} \quad (3.6)$$

Consequently, a brand owner who wants to have a greater share-in-shops-handling must either have (1) a higher turnover than its competitors, (2) more packages of its brand on the shelves than its competitors[9] or (3) both.

### Metric interpretation

The SISH shows the demand for a brand in stores where it is available. The SISH is different from market share, because while assessing interest in a brand, the SISH neglects sales force effectiveness in building a brand's availability (which is discussed in Sections 3.1.1 and 3.1.2), which strongly impacts market share. In other words, the SISH shows how strong a shopper's interest in a brand is, but does not take into account how easy it is for them to find a store offering the brand. For new brands, the SISH has a high prognostic value. Even if the current market share is low, but the brand's share-in-shops-handling is high, then one can expect that improving the brand's availability (increase in weighted distribution) should result in a significant increase in market share. In turn, the low value of the SISH for a new brand can mean either its low attractiveness for the final customer or the selection of the wrong distribution channel (store format).

While in the initial period after launching a new brand, its market share increases mainly because of rising numeric and weighted distribution, when a brand's availability improves, the importance of the SISH increases (Jones and Slater 2003). If intensive efforts to improve a brand's availability result in significant increases in its weighted distribution, and when it is growing faster than its market share, this is a visible sign that a brand's SISH is decreasing, which might suggest problems with the brand's visibility in stores or on the shelves. Another explanation for a decreasing SISH while growing weighted distribution might be entering geographical regions where the brand is still little known. It would probably be useful in this case to analyze the brand development index (see Appendix 4), and inventory turnover.

**Case**

*In 2015, True Match from L'Oréal, mentioned earlier in the chapter, had a share-in-shops-handling of 28.5% (100 ⋆ 0.06/0.21). At that time, the leader of the market had a share-in-shops-handling of 13.3%. In other words, in those stores in which True Match was available, its share of sales was nearly twice that of the leader (in the case of stores in which the leader was offered). In 2017, share-in-shops-handling of True Match increased to 34.6%. In other words, part of the market share rise could be explained by the increase in the brand's sales in the stores handling it.*

## 3.2 Buyer's perspective of brand sales

Having analyzed a brand's availability, its visibility in stores and how well it sells, the time has come to check how well the brand fares with consumers. We will analyze that using the trial purchase and penetration rates.

### *3.2.1 Trial purchase rate*

**Metric definition**

*Trial purchase rate* informs what proportion of category buyers has purchased a brand for the first time in a given time period.

**Metric calculation**

$$\text{Trial rate} = 100 \star \text{number of first-time brand buyers} : \text{number of product category buyers} \tag{3.7}$$

The data needed to calculate the trial rate can be derived from either surveys or (more reliably) consumer panels. As for the period of time that should be the basis for the analysis, the rule is quite simple – the more often the purchase of a given product category is repeated, the shorter the period of analysis (and vice versa). For products/services purchased on average every week, the shortest analysis period should be a quarter; for products purchased once every few weeks, the period of analysis should be one year (certainly not a quarter).

### Case

*Fixes are a popular category of ready-made meals in Poland. In mid-2006, two years after the brand's launch, 'Winiary Pomysl na' (which belongs to Nestle) reached 35.9% (among Fixes' consumers in Poland) (Effie Awards Album 2008, p. 19).*

### Metric interpretation

The availability of a new brand in a sufficiently large number of points of sale is just a prerequisite for its market success. Above all, encouraging potential buyers to make their first purchase is of paramount importance. A trial purchase is a measure of interest in a new brand, which is the effect of the buyer's natural curiosity and successful marketing activities, especially packaging and brand communication, with the exception of the product itself, which the buyer does not know yet. The level of arousal in a consumer's brain resulting from a stimulus in the form of the packaging of a new brand on the store shelf, as opposed to the arousal from a regularly purchased brand, is usually higher. In the case of FMCG, the favourable factor will usually be low price, which means that even if the customer's existing product inventory has not run out, he/she might still fancy purchasing a new yogurt just out of curiosity and because the brand is relatively cheap and has nice packaging. Of course, in the case of more expensive products/services, an unmet need is critical, as it prompts the buyer to look for a product to satisfy that need. All available research (but even common sense) indicates that *trial purchase determines the market success of a new brand*. Therefore, all the marketing activities of the brand's owner must be focused primarily on a trial's rapid growth. There is no chance for an increase in sales resulting from repeat purchases by satisfied customers if they have not purchased the brand in the first place.

Easier said than done. Powerful forces are working together against the new brand. On the one hand, inertia makes it safer, more convenient and more effortless for the consumer to buy brands that he/she already knows. Even if the buyer gets out of the default routine shopping mode, and realizes that a new brand has appeared in the category that he/she is shopping for at that moment (e.g. candies, red wines or cosmetic masks), the buyer notices at the same time that there are a few other new brands, and therefore the chances that he/she will choose ours is small by nature. And this is because of the impact of marketing by rival brands that also have attractive packaging and are supported by persuasive communication and numerous promotional incentives.

Market statistics show that new brands are now achieving much lower trial rates than in the past, which is due to the fact that many categories are already over-saturated with brands (resulting in fewer so-called market gaps related to unmet consumer needs), as well as the fact that consumers who had in the past eagerly reached for all new brands have realized that many of them pretend to offer any novelty. Under the new brand name, consumers tend to find an identical or almost identical product to the one they had already been buying. According to McKinsey (Haas et al. 2020), satisfaction rates for products offered as 'new' range across categories from 20% to 60%. Therefore, consumers have grown more reserved about new brands and their 'newness' effect.

The trial rate for a given brand can be compared with other brands that a company has launched previously on the market (in the same or a similar category), or newly introduced competitive brands (which can also be asked about in the survey).

### 3.2.2 Penetration rate

**Metric definition**

*Penetration rate* informs what proportion of category buyers has purchased a brand at least once in a given time period.

**Metric calculation**

$$\text{Penetration rate} = 100 \star \text{number of brand buyers, even if one-time} : \text{number of category buyers} \quad (3.8)$$

The optimal source of information for the analysis of penetration is consumer panels or the Target Group Index (TGI) survey. The penetration rate is usually analyzed on a quarterly, semi-annual or annual basis.

**Alternative way to calculate penetration rate**

In the absence of access to consumer panels, brand penetration can be calculated on the basis of information on the average number of packages of a given brand bought by its buyers and the total number of category buyers (both can be easily estimated on the basis of consumer surveys):

$$\text{Penetration rate} = \text{total number of brand packages sold} : \left(\begin{array}{l}\text{number of brand packages purchased by an average consumer} \\ \star \text{ number of buyers of the product category}\end{array}\right) \quad (3.9)$$

You can also calculate the penetration transforming formula (Formula 7.2):

$$\text{Penetration rate} = \text{market share} : (\text{share of wallet} * \text{heavy usage index})^{10} \quad (3.10)$$

**Metric interpretation**

*The penetration rate explains the differences in the market shares of brands in a given category*. When brands are growing, it is due to the increase in their penetration rate (Sharp 2012) and not their share of wallet (see Section 5.5). If brand X has a greater market share than brand Y (e.g. 10% vs. 5%), it is because it has greater penetration, and not because it has more loyal buyers or because they purchase larger quantities of the product. The importance of penetration for further brand growth decreases as its market share increases (McQueen et al. 1998). After exceeding the threshold of 10% of market share, the importance of a brand's penetration growth decreases and the importance of its share of wallet increases (Jones 1998). So, the superiority of penetration in growing a brand's market share relates to the short and medium time horizon. In the long term, most consumers have experience with purchasing many brands (even if only one-off), so the penetration rates of different brands do not differ greatly, and the brand's share of wallet starts to be of key importance[11] (Ehrenberg 1998). As shown in Figure 3.2, in each succeeding year, penetration (the sum of trialists and brand users from the previous year) is increasing and the cumulative percentage of lost customers is also growing. At the same time, the pool of non-trialists, in other words, those category users who have not tried the brand yet, is getting smaller and smaller. Consequently, the potential for penetration growth is running out, so the brand owner must turn its attention to retaining as many customers as possible (and maybe also getting back some of the lost ones).

The experience of consulting companies (Bain & Co. 2015) indicates that the condition for the success of a new brand is reaching a penetration rate of at least 15%. Singh and Wright (2016) suggest a simple rule for estimating the annual penetration rate for a new brand launched into the market. The trial rate reached in the first 13 weeks (a quarter) should be multiplied by 3. Increasing penetration is an effective strategy especially for brands just launched into the market, small brands (small market share), brands in new and fast-growing categories and service brands (Binet and Field 2007). Penetration is also particularly important in the case of frequently

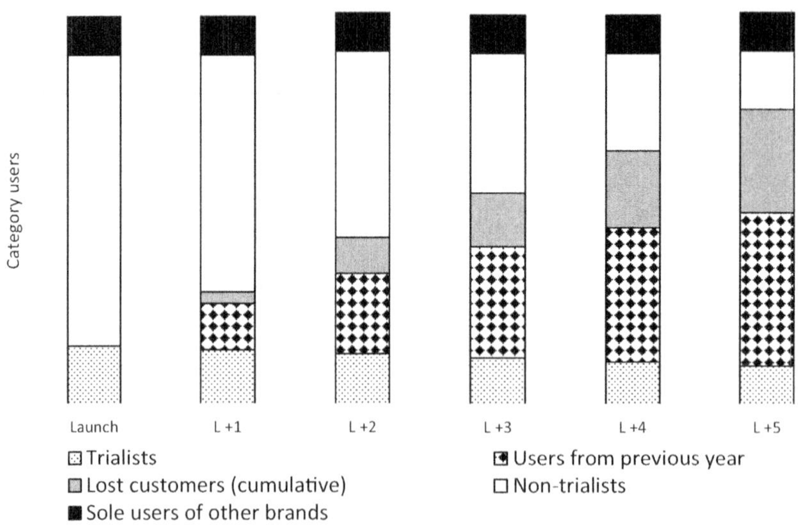


**DIAGRAM 3.1** Decreasing potential for penetration growth over time.

purchased goods (FMCG), whereby reaching more and more new buyers, penetration is constantly increasing (scores for the consecutive quarters or half-year periods increase), up to a specified, foreseeable maximum level (Jones and Slater 2003; Jones 1998). When the market matures and the brand is available over a long time period, its penetration rate for a specified time period (e.g. a quarter) begins to stabilize. And this is because we obtain the penetration rate by adding to first-time brand buyers those who know the brand from earlier purchases and those who repeat their behaviour. After the brand has been available for some time, the percentage of those first-time brand buyers decreases sharply (Diagram 3.1). On the other hand, the overwhelming majority of current brand customers stay with the brand.

### Case

*The penetration rates for succeeding 3- and 12-month periods, for three brands of beer in the Polish market*[12] *are shown in Tables 3.5 and 3.6.*

As the analyzed time period is lengthened, the penetration rate increases, but at a decreasing rate. In other words, the annual penetration rate is not four times, but, in fact, double or slightly more than the quarterly penetration rate. The reason behind the decreasing rate of penetration growth is that by extending the analyzed time period, we find fewer and fewer new buyers ready to purchase the brand. This can be portrayed as a brand's struggle with consumers' indifference, and sometimes a negative brand attitude (especially among those who are loyal to competing brands, or those who have abandoned a brand for some reason in the past, and they do not want to return to it). When taking into account penetration over a longer period of time (e.g. a year compared to a quarter), we increase the

**TABLE 3.5** Penetration rates for succeeding 12-month periods, in the case of selected beer brands in Poland (2018–2019)

| | *Q1 2018* | *Q2 2018* | *Q3 2018* | *Q4 2018* | *Q1 2019* | *Q2 2019* | *Q3 2019* | *Q4 2019* |
|---|---|---|---|---|---|---|---|---|
| Lech Premium | 41 | 37 | 36 | 35 | 36 | 36 | 38 | 39 |
| Tyskie Gronie | 37 | 38 | 38 | 37 | 39 | 39 | 41 | 39 |
| Zubr | 42 | 38 | 36 | 35 | 37 | 36 | 37 | 37 |

Source: Company data.

**TABLE 3.6** Penetration rates for succeeding three-month periods, in the case of selected beer brands in Poland (2018–2019)

| | *Q1 2018* | *Q2 2018* | *Q3 2018* | *Q4 2018* | *Q1 2019* | *Q2 2019* | *Q3 2019* | *Q4 2019* |
|---|---|---|---|---|---|---|---|---|
| Lech Premium | 25 | 23 | 22 | 21 | 20 | 21 | 23 | 23 |
| Tyskie Gronie | 25 | 26 | 26 | 24 | 25 | 26 | 29 | 25 |
| Zubr | 25 | 25 | 23 | 22 | 24 | 23 | 24 | 23 |

Source: Company data.

chance of finding one-off, 'random' buyers. But even strong, well-known brands often encounter an insurmountable barrier at the level of approximately 60% or 70% of category buyers, ready to buy the brand in question. As attractive and unique as brand X might be for its customers, for the rest of the market it is a less attractive alternative than the one they are currently buying, and therefore they will not increase brand X's penetration.

### Case

*Increases in the penetration rate, between monthly, quarterly and yearly, for three brands of beer in the Polish market are shown in Table 3.7.*

Researchers have found a relationship between the level of penetration and the strong emotions that buyers have towards a brand. In general, the higher the penetration, the weaker the so-called brand love (and vice versa) (Zarantonello et al. 2016). 'Brand love dilution', which takes place with the increase in the brand's penetration, is explained by the actions of the brand owner. Aiming at increasing the brand's reach within different market segments, the owner begins to consciously depart from the niche benefits that the brand used to offer its buyers, towards more mainstream ones. This results in customers starting to perceive the brand as less distinctive and unique, and newly acquired clients find that it offers basically the same benefits as many competing brands.

International comparisons of a brand's penetration rate allow determining the brand's growth potential in a given market. The explanation why in one market the same brand achieves (let's say) 40% penetration, and in another only 20% can be its different competitive position probably resulting from the presence of strong local brands, its different level of availability (measured by numeric and weighted distribution) or different tastes or consumer preferences (they will usually have a strong impact on food products). Regardless of the reason, the large regional diversity of brand penetration is a strong signal to intensify marketing activities and sales efforts in regions with lower penetration (see also Appendix 4).

### Cases

(1) *The global penetration of Intel's chip in the case of desktop computers was 84% in 2019 (Swanning in 2019).*

(2) *Snickers (which belongs to Mars) is one of the leading global brands of chocolate bars. In 2015, following the advertising campaign with Mr Bean ('Kung-Fu'), Snickers'*

**TABLE 3.7** Increase of penetration rates between a one-month and a one-year time frame, for three brands of Polish beer (2019)

| | *Monthly* | *Quarterly* | *Yearly* |
|---|---|---|---|
| Tyskie Gronie | 19 | 26 | 39 |
| Zubr | 17 | 23 | 37 |
| Lech Premium | 15 | 22 | 37 |

Source: Company data.

*penetration in Russia (one of the major markets for the brand) was 17.4% and in Australia it was 22.4% (Fenlon 2016).*

(3) *In 2017, penetration of DFS (mentioned in Chapter 2) among so-called 'quality seekers' (defined as those consumers who are prepared to pay a premium for a quality product) was 25% (Ross 2018).*

## Metric limitations

Sometimes, the reference point for calculating the penetration rate is not the number of product category buyers, but consumers in general. In such a case, penetration rates are lower, of course.

There is also the question of defining the product category itself: the narrower it is, the higher the penetration of the brand. Pepsi has higher penetration in the cola market than in carbonated drinks in general; even lower if by 'category' we mean drinks in general (see Section 1.1).

## Recommendations for brand managers

1. When measuring brand availability, weighted distribution is more important than numeric distribution. Too high numeric distribution accompanied by a relatively low level of weighted distribution signals inefficiencies in distributing the brand.
2. If the brand has low share-in-shops-handling, this is a signal of either low attractiveness for shoppers, or a mistake in the choice of retailers where the brand is offered. In such a case, increasing the numeric distribution will not be helpful.
3. When launching a new brand, a high trial rate is evidence of successful marketing activities, but not of high perceived quality of the product. It does not make sense to measure the trial rate for brands with a long history of market presence.
4. A condition for the success of a new brand is reaching a penetration rate of at least 15%, so initially all marketing activities should concentrate on acquiring new customers. In order to estimate the annual penetration rate for a new brand, you should multiply the trial rate in the first 13 weeks (a quarter) by 3.
5. A brand's market share grows because of an increase in the penetration rate, but penetration's importance decreases as a brand's market share increases.
6. Remember that brands with a high penetration rate cannot be 'loved' by every customer.

## Questions

1. Is the numeric distribution more important than the weighted one? Explain your answer.
2. How is a brand's share-in-shops-handling related to a brand's market share?
3. If we want to increase a brand's share-in-shops-handling, is there an alternative to increasing a brand's turnover?

4. Why is a trial purchase an important metric when launching new brands?
5. Why is the penetration rate crucial for explaining a brand's market share?
6. Can a brand with a high penetration rate evoke strong positive emotions among all its buyers?

## Notes

1 According to Bain & Co., leading consumer packaged goods manufacturers have distribution and transportation costs below 6% of their revenue, while the typical range is 6%–8% (Ruffin et al. 2018).

2 In some countries, e.g. Poland, huge numbers of retail stores operate. According to the Polish Central Statistical Office, about 340,000 stores exist, almost 90% of which have a selling area below 100 m$^2$.

3 In the UK, four chains, namely Tesco, Sainsbury's, ASDA and Morrison's, have dominated almost 70% of the FMCG retail market (27%, 15.4%, 14.9% and 10.1% share, respectively). In 2019, their share slightly decreased compared to 2012 (30.9%, 16.4%, 17.5% and 11.5%, respectively). Source: Statista 2020.

4 Like Poland, where more than 40% of grocery sales takes place in small grocery stores, of which there are just over 90,000 (Nielsen 2018). The situation is even more complex in some African countries – according to Nielsen (2015), in Ghana, Cameroon and Nigeria, at least 96% of sales is generated through traditional trade. In 2016, Bain & Co. consultants estimated that tiny shops in China accounted for at least 40% of FMCG sales (Root Xing 2016).

5 The denominator is the result of dividing the percentage of sales realized by stations where the brand is not available by the percentage share of such stations.

6 That we can conclude from the division of their weighted distributions (51/11.3).

7 For example, in 2018, in its home market of the United States, McDonald's had double the number of outlets of Burger King (The Whopper Detour 2020).

8 Inventory turns inform how many times (in a given period of time) the average brand inventory available on store shelves is sold.

Inventory turns = number of brand packages sold: average number of brand packages available on shelves

Note that the volume and the frequency of brand deliveries to a given retailer are usually known to the brand owner so they can be used to calculate the number of packages sold in a given period of time. And an average number of brand packages on the shelves of stores can be easily determined by sales representatives.

Transforming the above formula, we arrive at another approach to calculate turnover:

Inventory turns = 100 * brand's share-in-shops-handling * category sales: average number of brand packages on the shelves

Inventory turns can also be calculated based on 'inventory days' which is the average number of days of a brand's inventory carried by a retailer:

*Inventory turns = 365: inventory days*

Inventory turns show the level of interest in the brand among shoppers and the quality of its merchandizing. It is obvious that high relative (compared with rival brands) turns prove that the brand sells faster and thus the retailer will probably be interested in ordering it. Inventory turns are affected by brand strength, relative price and, in the case of lesser known brands, eye-catching packaging. A decrease in a brand's inventory turns at a given retail chain usually foretells problems with convincing the retailer to keep the brand on its shelves. For retailers, the business terms offered by a supplier (margins, discounts, terms of payment) and a brand's inventory turns are key variables for assessing the profitability of handling a given brand.

9 We cannot expect that brand merchandizing will influence the decision of a shopper who has already decided what brand of coffee, washing powder or olive oil he/she

intends to buy. This is especially true for shoppers buying only one, favourite brand (sole brand users – see Section 5.3). But in categories that are less important for the shopper, where he/she has not much experience with brands, the number of facings may, to some extent, determine the sales of the brand. Yet, only those packages on the shelves that are facing the buyer ('facings') can influence his/her decision-making process. It is difficult to expect that packages scattered over the shelves, partly overturned and partly with a label turned back, could affect the purchasing decision. Van Nierop et al. (2008) have proved that an increase in the number of facings causes an increase in sales, although the marginal sales increase caused by adding an extra facing is decreasing. This is confirmed by analyses of Drèze et al. (1994), who additionally state that at some point (different for various products) the sales increase from additional facings becomes zero. In addition, they emphasize that positioning a brand on a shelf is more important than the number of facings. Chandon et al. (2009) very precisely determined (using, among others, eye-tracking research) the impact of increasing the number of facings on noticing the brand and its consideration. For occasional buyers of a brand with a small market share, doubling the number of facings improves brand recognition by 26%, brand consideration by 22% and brand purchase by 67%. For brands with average market shares, the effects are generally smaller: brand consideration and selection increase by only 10%. Of course, the research covered selected product categories, and within them specific brands, and finally it was conducted in specific store formats. It is impossible to consider those increases to be universal (guaranteed for every brand, at every store). Since the number of facings is so important (especially in the case of FMCG), one should analyze the strength of the brand's impact on a shopper by the brand's share of shelf, calculated as follows:

Brand share of shelf = 100 * number of brand facings: the total number of facings

A brand's share of shelf is a metric of a brand's display prominence. It should roughly correspond to a brand's relative share-in-shops-handling. However, it also depends on both the strength of a brand owner's relationship with a given retail chain and the financial incentives offered (especially in the case of new brands). For a brand entering a retail chain (especially for a brand with a significant market share), its market share should certainly be an argument in negotiating its share of shelf.

10 Heavy usage index can be omitted as it is usually close to 1 (see: chapter 7.2).

11 Let us analyze the smartphone market, not on a yearly basis, but e.g. 10 years. A significant part of the brands currently available on the market have been purchased in this period at least once, by a significant percentage of smartphone buyers, which is why the differences in their penetration rates (remember we are talking about a 10 year horizon) is not large. Therefore, the differences in market shares are better explained by the differences in share of wallet (in 10 years) of each of the competing brands.

12 All the information in this chapter, regarding that case has been delivered by the Consumer Insights Team of Kompania Piwowarska.

## Literature

Ataman M.B., Van Heerde J.L, Mela C.F., 2010, The Long-Term Effect of Marketing Strategy on Brand Sales, *Journal of Marketing Research*, XLVII, pp. 866–882, doi: 10.1509/jmkr.47.5.866.

Bain, 2019, https://www.bain.com/insights/what-consumers-want-from-online-grocery-shopping-wsj/ [access: 10.10.2020].

BCG, 2020, https://www.bcg.com/publications/2020/cpg-companies-face-increased-e-commerce [access; 12.10. 2020].

Binet L., Field P., 2007, *Marketing in the Era of Accountability: Identifying the Marketing Practices and Metrics That Truly Increase Profitability*, World Advertising Research Center, Henley-on-Thames.

Bisnode, 2019, www.bisnode.pl/wiedza/newsy-artykuly/wzrost-liczby-sklepow-internetowych-w-polsce-w-pierwszym-polroczu-2019-r/ [access: 6.06.2020].

Chandon P., Hutchinson J.W., Bradlow E.T., Young S.H., 2009, Does In-Store Marketing Work? Effects of the Number and Position of Shelf Facings on Brand Attention and Evaluation at the Point of Purchase, *Journal of Marketing*, 73(6), pp. 1–17, doi: 10.1509/jmkg.73.6.1.

Drèze X., Hoch S.J., Purk M.E., 1994, Shelf Management and Space Elasticity, *Journal of Retailing*, 70(4), pp. 301–326 doi: 10.1016/0022-4359(94)90002-7.

Edelstein P., Davey K.S., Gupta A., Sarcus S., Brennan J., Loeys C., *What the Fastest-Growing CPG Companies Do Differently*, BCG, 14 June, www.bcg.com/pl-pl/publications/2018/what-fastest-growing-consumer-packaged-goods-companies-do-differently [access; 7.01.2021].

*Effie Awards Album*, 2008, Stowarzyszenie Komunikacji Marketingowej, Warszawa.

Ehrenberg A.S.C., 1998, Repetitive Advertising and the Consumer, in: *How Advertising Works: The Role of Research*, ed. J.Ph. Jones, SAGE, Thousand Oaks, pp. 63–81.

Ellis E., Frymann D., Kouralis V., 2018, How L'Oréal Paris UK True Match Climbed to No. 1 by Making Everyone Feel 'Worth it', in: *Advertising Works 24: Proving the Payback on Marketing Investment*, ed. N. Godber, Institute of Practitioners in Advertising + WARC, London, pp. 253–282.

Fenlon E., 2016, Snickers: Thinking Like a Hollywood Blockbuster, in: *Advertising Works 23: Proving the Payback on Marketing Investment*, ed. B. Angear, Institute of Practitioners in Advertising + WARC, London, pp. 283–302.

Gallery R., Sor L., 2016, Guinness: An Effectiveness Story Made of More, in: *Advertising Works 23: Proving the Payback on Marketing Investment*, ed. B. Angear, Institute of Practitioners in Advertising + WARC, London, pp.165–208.

Haas S., McClain J., McInerney P., Timelin B., 2020, *Reimagining Consumer-Goods Innovation for the Next Normal*, "Our Insights McKinsey and Company", 16 October.

Jones J.Ph., 1998, Penetration, Brand Loyalty, and the Penetration Supercharge, in: *How Advertising Works: The Role of Research*, ed. J.Ph. Jones, SAGE, Thousand Oaks, pp. 57–62.

Jones J.Ph., Slater J.S., 2003, *What's In a Name?* Advertising and the Concept of Brands, M.E. Sharpe, Armonk.

McQueen J., Sylvester A.K., Moore S.D., 1998, Brand Growth: The Past, the Present, in: *How Advertising Works: The Role of Research*, ed. J.Ph. Jones, SAGE, Thousand Oaks, pp. 49–56.

Nielsen, 2015, *Africa: How to Navigate the Retail Distribution Labyrinth*, February, The Nielsen Company.

Nielsen, 2018, *Poland Shopper Trends 2018/2019*, The Nielsen Company.

Quarterly Retail E-Commerce Sales 3rd Quarter, 2020, *U.S. Census Bureau News*, U.S. Department of Commerce, Washington, 19 November.

Root J., Xing W., 2016, China's Deteriorating Retail Distribution System, *Wall Street Journal*, 17 October, www.wsj.com/articles/chinas-deteriorating-retail-distribution-system-1476722869 [access: 11.12.2020].

Ross A., 2018, Turning DFS from a Value Brand into a Brand That People Value, in: *Advertising Works 24: Proving the Payback on Marketing Investment*, ed. N. Godber, Institute of Practitioners in Advertising + WARC, London, pp. 113–156.

Ruffin R., Shehorn M., Banerjee D., Lapin J., 2018, *Are Your Distribution and Transportation Costs Out of Control?* Bain & Co. Brief, 11 September www.bain.com/insights/are-your-distribution-and-transportation-costs-out-of-control/ [access: 7.01.2021]

Sharp B., 2012, *How Brands Grow: What Marketers Don't Know*, Oxford University Press Australia, Oxford University Press.

Singh J., Wright M., 2016, New Brands: Performance and Measurement, in: *The Routledge Companion to Contemporary Brand Management*, ed. F. Dall'Olmo Riley, J. Singh, Ch. Blankson, Routledge, London, pp. 186–199.

Srinivasan S., Vanhuele M., Pauwels K., 2008, Do Mindset Metrics Explain Brand Sales?, *MSI Reports Working Paper Series, Issue Four, 08–004*, pp. 47–67.

Statista, 2020, www.statista.com/statistics/300656/grocery-market-share-in-great-britain-year-on-year-comparison/ [access: 30.12.2020].

Swanning in, 2019, *The Economist*, 9 February.

The Whopper Detour, 2020, *Effie Awards United States Gold Winner Case Study*, Effie Worldwide, Inc., New York.

van Nierop E., Fok D., Franses Ph.H., 2008, Interaction Between Shelf Layout and Marketing Effectiveness and its Impact on Optimizing Shelf Arrangements, *Marketing Science*, 27(6), pp. 1065–1082.

Vishwanath V., Delaney L., Meacham M., Tager S., 2014, *Winning with Brands: What Will It Take to Keep Brands Thriving Bain And Company Brief*, 24 June, www.bain.com/insights/winning-with-brands/ [access: 10.10.2020].

Wiadomosci Handlowe, 2019, www.wiadomoscihandlowe.pl/artykuly/rynek-stacji-paliw-w-polsce-w-i-kw-2019-r-struktur,54022 [access: 5.06.2020].

Zarantonello L., Formisano M., Grappi S., 2016, The Relationship between Brand Love and Actual Brand Performance: Evidence from an International Study, *International Marketing Review*, 33(6), pp. 806–824, doi: 10.1108/IMR-11-2015-0238.

# 4

# MEASURING POST-PURCHASE EVALUATION

**Learning objectives:**

After reading this chapter you should

- understand the concept of satisfaction and why it is always relative;
- be aware of problems with measuring satisfaction;
- be familiar with three satisfaction metrics: Customer Satisfaction Index (CSI), Weighted Satisfaction Index (WSI) and Net Promoter Score (NPS);
- be able to calculate all of the above metrics;
- recognize the limitations of a very popular metric, which is the NPS.

An important stage in a customer's journey begins after the brand purchase. The buyer begins consuming the product/service and finds that the experience delivered by the brand is satisfactory (problem solved or reward supplied) or it is not. At this stage, with the exception of the product and the accompanying services (e.g. repairs), other marketing instruments become of minor importance.

We intuitively understand the importance of satisfied customers for a brand's future success. As long as a customer has a choice, he/she will not continue buying a brand that does not satisfy. Therefore, the need to analyze customer satisfaction seems obvious. The more so, as most surveys clearly demonstrate the relationship between improving customer satisfaction and the economic performance of the brand owner (Gupta and Zeithaml 2006). It is worth mentioning that this relationship is asymmetrical, which means that a 1% decrease in satisfaction causes relatively more harm than the benefits of a 1% increase in satisfaction. This is because many customers seem to take satisfaction for granted. Customers will barely notice if you improve the Customer Satisfaction Index by 1%, but lowering it by 1% will have an impact. Additionally, we know that the

DOI: 10.4324/9781003167235-4

relationship between satisfaction and a company's economic results is non-linear and varies for different industries – it is probably stronger for services with a high level of risk than for tangible goods – and even more so between various companies in the same industry.

## 4.1 Satisfaction defined

**Definition**: *Satisfaction is an emotional reaction resulting from a comparison of a customer's brand experience with his/her expectations. Customer satisfaction comes from the experience provided by the brand exceeding his/her expectations.*

At this point, it should be clear that satisfaction is purely subjective. It is *not* an evaluation of the objective quality of a product or service. Since satisfaction depends on the buyer's expectations, it may turn out that he/she is, for example, more satisfied with a meal in a cheap fast-food restaurant (most likely expectations regarding food and service are not too high in the first place) than with tasting a menu in an expensive restaurant where, objectively speaking, both the service and the food are incomparably better. The problem is that the consumer might have expected more.

The measurement of brand satisfaction is always, in a natural way, *relative*: consumers always perceive different objects in relation to others. They show a natural tendency not only to compare things with each other but also to concentrate comparisons on easily comparable objects (Ariely 2009).

## 4.2 Problems with satisfaction measurement

There are several problems with measuring satisfaction. Let's start with the obvious one: it can be *understood differently*. First, a distinction should be made between overall and episodic/partial satisfaction. Overall satisfaction is taken from a whole set of experiences resulting from the purchase and consumption of a brand, while partial satisfaction concerns the individual stages of purchasing or consuming, or satisfaction from the individual attributes of a product/service. Secondly, current or cumulative satisfaction can be measured. Current satisfaction refers to the last act of purchasing or consuming a brand, and cumulative satisfaction covers the accumulated experiences with a brand over a longer period of time (Gupta and Zeithaml 2006).

Finally (and this is rarely raised), satisfaction can refer to current or time-shifted comparisons with other brands. Current satisfaction applies to products/services of which the customer is using at least two brands simultaneously, which is common in B2B markets. In this case, a customer can assess brand satisfaction against that of rivals. Satisfaction 'shifted in time' applies to products/services of which a customer uses only one brand at a time, which is common in B2C markets, especially in the case of goods/services with a high unit price (the majority of consumers will purchase just one home from one developer at a time and take out just one insurance policy), or in the case of specific services (such as electricity or gas supply – in this case, it is difficult to use the services of different suppliers at the same time), or in quasi-monopolistic markets (such as public transport in a given city – in this case, brand satisfaction may only be compared to brands whose consumption took place earlier [oftentimes, much earlier]). This shift in time, due to the natural phenomena of forgetting and continuously deconstructing and recreating memories, makes the measurement of relative satisfaction with the currently used brand against the background of previously used brands largely distorted by imperfect memory.

Next in the measurement of satisfaction, an important question arises: 'whom to survey?'. Respondents in a satisfaction survey may be

(1) Heavy brand users (e.g. the top 20% are usually responsible for half of a brand's consumption; East et al. 2008): sole brand users do not have an ongoing experience with other brands, and thus will not assess the brand against competitors; we should take for granted that their satisfaction is high (otherwise, they would look for other brands).
(2) Average, typical users of a brand: the brand is usually one of a few purchased brands (repertoire of brands; see Section 5.2), so these respondents have a reference point and their opinions might be the most 'objective'.
(3) Occasional brand users: for some reason (seldom known to the brand owner) they purchase the brand rarely/in small quantities; they may have a vague sense of brand performance.
(4) New buyers who have their first experience with the brand (in their case, you cannot ask for cumulative satisfaction).

Moreover, the above four groups can be further categorized due to the intensity of a product's consumption. It is known that the expectations of those consumers with more product experience are higher (Stasiuk and Maison 2014). Of course, nothing stands in the way (it would even be advisable) of carrying out research in all segments, but this will increase the cost of the survey.

It is important to remember the careful selection of the sample that would represent the surveyed population. For example, instead of laying out questionnaire forms in hotel rooms or at the reception desk, with the expectation that many of the guests will decide to fill them in, it is better to choose respondents on a random basis, for example, ask every fifth hotel guest to fill in the questionnaire while checking out. In the former case, it is very likely that there will be a kind of sample self-selection and the survey will only be completed by customers who are dissatisfied with the hotel services (their motivation is stronger as a result of their emotional state), which will significantly distort the results of the measurement.

The place and time of conducting the interviews are also important, as these affect, among others, the length of the questionnaire (number of attributes to be evaluated). It is difficult to ask hotel guests who are checking out to complete a survey evaluating 20 components of the services offered.

Surveys can be carried out immediately after the service/product has been delivered when the respondent has a vivid memory of it. The advantage is the spontaneity of the evaluation, not being falsified by a volatile memory. The alternative is to survey customers after some time has passed from when they started using a product/service, allowing the customer to express calculated and thoughtful opinions.

Having in mind all of the aforementioned dilemmas, we can measure customer satisfaction using one of three metrics: Customer Satisfaction Index, Weighted Satisfaction Index or Net Promoter Score.

## 4.3 Customer Satisfaction Index

**Metric definition**

*Customer Satisfaction Index* is the overall evaluation of a brand on those of its attributes that are significant to customers, without taking into consideration the attributes' varying degrees of importance to customers.

If you do not have knowledge of the relative importance for the customer of various product attributes or service delivery areas, you must assume that they are all equally important. Thus, the Customer Satisfaction Index is calculated as follows:

**Metric calculation**

$$\text{Customer Satisfaction Index} = \frac{\text{sum of average ratings in all attributes against which brand is evaluated}}{\text{number of attributes}} \quad (4.1)$$

The research process itself requires, in the first instance, to determine the key factors that have an impact on overall customer satisfaction. To do this, it is best to conduct qualitative research, e.g. focus group interviews or individual in-depth interviews. Subsequently, some scale should be adopted (e.g. from 1 to 5; from −3 to +3; or 'very dissatisfied – rather dissatisfied – neither satisfied nor dissatisfied – rather satisfied – very satisfied'), always bearing in mind that an odd number of variants (with a 'middle' rating, interpreted as 'neither satisfied nor dissatisfied') should be applied.

**Example**

The manager of a chain of roadside motels has decided to ask every fifth guest at check-out, how they evaluate various attributes of the motel. Before preparing the survey questionnaire, he consulted trade publications, articles regarding customer satisfaction and guests' comments on sites such as TripAdvisor, Yelp and the like. The final list of attributes has been talked through with the customers during two focus group interviews. Table 4.1 presents the distribution of answers. How should we calculate the Customer Satisfaction Index?

In the first place, we need to calculate the averages for all attributes (last column in Table 4.1), add them up and divide the sum by the number of attributes:

$$\text{CSI} = \left(4.07 + 2.95 + 2.66 + 3.2 + 4.25 + 2.13 + 4.46 + 4.69 + 4.54\right)/9$$

$$= 3.66$$

### Metric interpretation

As to the interpretation, one may find the suggestion to take just the 'top 2 boxes' of the 5-point scale (Bendle et al. 2015). Adding the percentages of these two boxes (either 'very satisfied' and '[rather] satisfied' or '5' and '4') is, of course, easier and faster than calculating the average (the more so, if it is the weighted average covered in Section 4.4). Yet, the conclusions drawn from the 'top 2 boxes' analysis might be very misleading. An example in Table 4.2 helps to understand why.

Let's say we have the distribution of responses by customers of brands X and Y (competing in the same category). If we use the 'top 2 boxes' formula, then one might conclude that both brands have been satisfying customers at the same level. Yet, the average will unmistakably show that customers' satisfaction in the case of brand X is much higher than in the case of brand Y. And if we look at the distribution of scores, we will understand why.

**TABLE 4.1** Hypothetical ratings of motels X

| *Attributes* | *Very satisfied (5) (%)* | *Rather satisfied (4) (%)* | *Neither satisfied nor dissatisfied (3) (%)* | *Rather dissatisfied (2) (%)* | *Very dissatisfied (1) (%)* | *Average** |
|---|---|---|---|---|---|---|
| Service at receptionist desk | 34 | 39 | 27 | 0 | 0 | 4.07 |
| Comfort of the bed | 11 | 21 | 26 | 36 | 6 | 2.95 |
| Room furnishings | 0 | 18 | 39 | 34 | 9 | 2.66 |
| Bathroom furnishings | 14 | 19 | 44 | 19 | 4 | 3.2 |
| General cleanliness | 51 | 31 | 11 | 6 | 1 | 4.25 |
| Tranquility | 10 | 13 | 12 | 10 | 55 | 2.13 |
| Breakfast | 61 | 24 | 15 | 0 | 0 | 4.46 |
| Ease of driving to | 73 | 23 | 4 | 0 | 0 | 4.69 |
| Parking possibilities | 64 | 29 | 4 | 3 | 0 | 4.54 |

* For example, for 'service at the receptionist desk' we calculate partial satisfaction as follows: (0.34*5) + (0.39*4) + (0.27*3) = 4.07.

**TABLE 4.2** A case of two brands with identical 'top 2 boxes' and different CSI scores

| *Brand* | *'1'* | *'2'* | *'3'* | *'4'* | *'5'* | *Top 2 boxes (%)* | *CSI* |
|---|---|---|---|---|---|---|---|
| X | 5 | 10 | 20 | 30 | 35 | **65** | **3.80** |
| Y | 20 | 5 | 10 | 50 | 15 | **65** | **3.35** |

On the other hand, we cannot rely on the CSI alone and should always consult the distribution of scores, which is clearly explained in Table 4.3.

If we analyze in detail the distribution of the answers, we have two brands with the same CSI (3.60) and the same 'top 2 boxes' (60%), yet totally different levels of satisfaction. Of brand Y customers, 25% are totally dissatisfied with the brand, yet half of them are fully satisfied. Brand X has a very low percentage of unsatisfied customers ('1' and '2') – just 5% in total. The majority of its customers (85%) are rather mildly satisfied ('3' or '4'). Even if both brands have the same CSI values and 'top 2 boxes', it looks as though brand Y does a much better job of satisfying its customers (half of them are fully satisfied), although not all of them. Brand managers should either meticulously examine the reasons for the dissatisfaction of a quarter of their customers, or target their marketing more precisely at those who find brand Y very satisfying, and try to increase their spending. The manager of brand X should concentrate efforts on improving customer experiences with the brand, to improve customer satisfaction. Today, brand X evokes just lukewarm feelings.

**Case**

*FIBARO,[1] headquartered near Poznan (Poland), has 10 years of experience in manufacturing smart home devices and, since July 2018, is part of the Nice Group. FIBARO's products are available on six continents and its unique customer value proposition is the fact that its devices are designed, developed and manufactured entirely in Poland. At the end of 2018, the management decided to measure the satisfaction of its end users, both in Poland and abroad. At the time of the survey, customers had been using FIBARO's devices for at least half a year (97% of foreign and 84% of local customers), with the majority having at least one-year brand experience (85% of foreign and 69% of local users). The Customer Satisfaction Index was based on five areas (product assortment, distributor's and installer's service, technical support and complaints handling). The CSI on a 5-point scale was 3.7 and 3.53 in the case of Polish customers and foreign customers, respectively. In both cases, the most satisfying was the installer's service (3.93 and 3.91, respectively) and the lowest was complaints handling.*

**Metric limitations**

The CSI is used to measure satisfaction with a brand, especially in services and B2B industries and in durable goods. It should not be used in the case of frequently purchased products (fast-moving consumer goods [FMCG]), which will be explained later.

Using the CSI, we arbitrarily assume that each of the factors determining customer satisfaction holds the same importance for the customer (therefore we give these factors the same weight). That assumption shortens the questionnaire and

**TABLE 4.3** A case of two brands with identical 'top 2 boxes' and CSI values but different distribution of scores

| *Brand* | *'1'* | *'2'* | *'3'* | *'4'* | *'5'* | *CSI* | *Top 2 boxes (%)* |
|---|---|---|---|---|---|---|---|
| X | 5 | 0 | 35 | 50 | 10 | **3.60** | **60** |
| Y | 25 | 0 | 15 | 10 | 50 | **3.60** | **60** |

concurrently simplifies the measurement. It is wiser, therefore, to analyze the relative importance (weight) of the selected attributes that should be determined, preferably using quantitative research (consumer survey), and then we obtain the Weighted Satisfaction Index (see Section 4.4).

Finally, when interpreting the Customer Satisfaction Index, we should remember that values slightly above average on the adopted scale (e.g. 3 on a 5-point scale) should be treated as actual average values! Of note, 3.2 or 3.3 on a 5-point scale is not a rating of a satisfied but rather a *polite* customer. Especially when the survey is completed in the presence of a company representative, respondents tend, to put it mildly, to slightly overrate the brand. Of course, this is strongly driven by culture so the magnitude of this effect will be different in different regions. This is confirmed by numerous studies, according to which the number of positive opinions appearing on the internet exceeds the number of negative opinions by 2.5 or even 3.5 times, on average (East et al. 2008). Analysis by reviewtrackers.com (2018) suggests that the share of positive opinions is growing, with the average rating (on a 5-point scale) increasing from 3.8 in 2010 to 4.25 in 2018, which means that rather than vent their disappointment with brands, consumers use the internet to review brands that have satisfied them. The opinion of some managers that customers are always extremely demanding and malicious and have many claims is probably overexaggerated. To find more on this, just check hotel reviews in any major European city on TripAdvisor, booking.com or a similar platform. The vast majority of hotels score at least 3 on a 5-point scale.

## 4.4 Weighted Satisfaction Index

### Metric definition

*Weighted Satisfaction Index* is the overall evaluation of a brand on those of its attributes that are significant to customers, taking into consideration their varying importance for customers.

If research was carried out to determine the weight of individual factors in building total brand satisfaction, then the formula for the Weighted Satisfaction Index would look as follows:

### Metric calculation

$$\text{Weighted Satisfaction Index} = \text{sum}\left(\text{partial satisfaction in each attribute} \star \text{weight of given attribute}\right) \quad (4.2)$$

if the sum of weights equals 1 or

$$\text{Weighted Satisfaction Index} = \text{sum}\left(\text{partial satisfaction in each attribute} * \text{weight of given attribute}\right) : \text{sum of weights} \quad (4.3)$$

if the sum of weights is different from 1.

**Example**

To see how the Weighted Satisfaction Index is calculated, imagine the situation where a manager of a chain of roadside motels has decided to add questions regarding the importance of selected attributes for guests. The distribution of answers is shown in Table 4.4.

The head of marketing of the motel chain has read about the 'top 2 boxes' approach and has decided to use it in this case. He calculates the average percentage of 'very satisfied' and 'rather satisfied' customers, adds them up and gets 59.4% of customers. He then concludes that, generally, the level of guest satisfaction is high, because on average almost 60% of guests are satisfied with their stay, and only every fifth is dissatisfied. Therefore, he believes that, in general, the motel chain owners should be happy with the metric. Is that conclusion correct?

By calculating the Weighted Satisfaction Index, we can more deeply understand the satisfaction of the guests of that motel chain. In order to arrive at that metric, you first need to calculate the weight of each attribute (we will make their sum equal to 1, thereby using Formula 4.2). Then, you multiply the partial satisfaction of each attribute by the corresponding weight and add them up (see Table 4.5).

$$\begin{aligned}
&\text{Weighted Satisfaction Index}\\
&\quad = (4.07 \star 0.1) + (2.95 \star 0.135) + (2.66 \star 0.108)\\
&\quad\ + (3.2 \star 0.118) + (4.25 \star 0.101) + (2.13 \star 0.128) + (4.46 \star 0.115)\\
&\quad\ + (4.69 \star 0.089) + (4.54 \star 0.106) = \mathbf{3.58}
\end{aligned}$$

As you can see, the Weighted Satisfaction Index is even lower than the CSI (3.66). It should therefore be concluded that customer satisfaction in this case is a bit above average, at best. Certainly, this is not a score that suggests that nothing needs to be improved. A detailed analysis of the level of satisfaction and the weight of each attribute shows a somewhat complicated picture (see Figure 4.1).

It is clear that only one important attribute of the stay, namely breakfast, nearly perfectly satisfies customers (4.46 on a 5-point scale). There are a few attributes that are relatively less important to customers, and the motel chain delivers them well above average. In this hypothetical example, for those looking for accommodation after a long drive, the issue of easy access to the motel turned out to be the least important (2.95), and at the same time the motel is rated relatively highest on this one (4.69). The situation is similar in three other areas: parking possibilities, room cleanliness and reception service. Those are not (according to our hypothetical research) key factors for overall customer satisfaction, and in their case the chain performs well above average. However, in three other attributes: silence during the night, bed comfort and bathroom furnishings, guests' expectations were above average (respectively, 4.21, 4.47 and 3.88),

**TABLE 4.4** Hypothetical ratings of motels X and importance of individual attributes

| *Attribute* | *Importance for guests* | | | | | *Ratings of motels* | | | | |
|---|---|---|---|---|---|---|---|---|---|---|
| | *Extremely important (5) (%)* | *Rather important (4) (%)* | *Neither important nor unimportant (3) (%)* | *Rather unimportant (2) (%)* | *Extremely unimportant (1) (%)* | *Very satisfied (5) (%)* | *Rather satisfied (4) (%)* | *Neither satisfied nor dissatisfied (3) (%)* | *Rather dissatisfied (2) (%)* | *Very dissatisfied (1) (%)* |
| Service at receptionist desk | 19 | 26 | 30 | 17 | 8 | 34 | 39 | 27 | 0 | 0 |
| Comfort of the bed | 62 | 23 | 15 | 0 | 0 | 11 | 21 | 26 | 36 | 6 |
| Room furnishings | 17 | 32 | 41 | 10 | 0 | 0 | 18 | 39 | 34 | 9 |
| Bathroom furnishings | 39 | 26 | 24 | 6 | 5 | 14 | 19 | 44 | 19 | 4 |
| General cleanliness | 21 | 29 | 26 | 9 | 15 | 51 | 31 | 11 | 6 | 1 |
| Tranquility | 50 | 33 | 9 | 4 | 4 | 10 | 13 | 12 | 10 | 55 |
| Breakfast | 41 | 21 | 21 | 11 | 6 | 61 | 24 | 15 | 0 | 0 |
| Ease of driving to | 11 | 26 | 26 | 21 | 16 | 73 | 23 | 4 | 0 | 0 |
| Parking possibilities | 35 | 20 | 17 | 15 | 13 | 64 | 29 | 4 | 3 | 0 |
| Average | | | | | | 35.3 | 24.1 | 20.2 | 12 | 8.3 |

**TABLE 4.5** Calculation of Weighted Satisfaction Index

| *Attribute* | *Importance for guests* | | | | | | | *Ratings of motels* | | | | | |
|---|---|---|---|---|---|---|---|---|---|---|---|---|---|
| | *Extremely important (5) (%)* | *Rather important (4) (%)* | *Neither important nor unimportant (3) (%)* | *Rather unimportant (2) (%)* | *Extremely unimportant (1) (%)* | *Average importance* | *Weight* | *Very satisfied (5) (%)* | *Rather satisfied (4) (%)* | *Neither satisfied nor dissatisfied (3) (%)* | *Rather dissatisfied (2) (%)* | *Very dissatisfied (1) (%)* | *Average satisfaction* |
| Service at receptionist desk* | 19 | 26 | 30 | 17 | 8 | **3.31** | 0.100 | 34 | 39 | 27 | 0 | 0 | **4.07** |
| Comfort of the bed | 62 | 23 | 15 | 0 | 0 | **4.47** | 0.135 | 11 | 21 | 26 | 36 | 6 | **2.95** |
| Room furnishings | 17 | 32 | 41 | 10 | 0 | **3.56** | 0.108 | 0 | 18 | 39 | 34 | 9 | **2.66** |
| Bathroom furnishings | 39 | 26 | 24 | 6 | 5 | **3.88** | 0.118 | 14 | 19 | 44 | 19 | 4 | **3.20** |
| General cleanliness | 21 | 29 | 26 | 9 | 15 | **3.32** | 0.101 | 51 | 31 | 11 | 6 | 1 | **4.25** |
| Tranquility | 50 | 33 | 9 | 4 | 4 | **4.21** | 0.128 | 10 | 13 | 12 | 10 | 55 | **2.13** |
| Breakfast | 41 | 21 | 21 | 11 | 6 | **3.8** | 0.115 | 61 | 24 | 15 | 0 | 0 | **4.46** |
| Ease of access | 11 | 26 | 26 | 21 | 16 | **2.95** | 0.089 | 73 | 23 | 4 | 0 | 0 | **4.69** |
| Parking possibilities | 35 | 20 | 17 | 15 | 13 | **3.49** | 0.106 | 64 | 29 | 4 | 3 | 0 | **4.54** |
| Total | | | | | | **32.99** | 1 | | | | | | |

* An example of calculating the average importance for service at the receptionist desk: 0.19*5 + 0.26*4 + 0.3*3 + 0.17*2 + 0.08*1 = 3.31. An example of calculating the average rating for service at the receptionist desk: 0.34*5 + 0.39 + 4 + 0.27*3 = 4.07. An example of calculating the weight for service at the receptionist desk: 3.31/32.99 = 0.100.

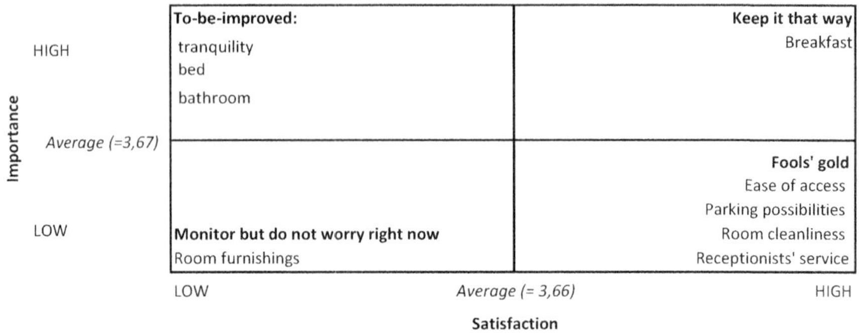


**FIGURE 4.1** Analysis of motels' customer satisfaction – what should we do?

and the level of satisfaction lower than average (significantly lower in the case of silence at 2.13). In other words, that brand of motels does not even fairly satisfy guests on those three key dimensions. The last attribute (room furnishings) is not rated highly (2.66), but it is also of relatively low importance (3.56). Therefore, you may not pay much attention to it today, but you should certainly monitor the expectations of guests in the future (which may increase even if impacted by nights slept in other motels).

### Metric interpretation

According to Morgan and Rego (2006), among the various metrics related to customer satisfaction, the *Weighted Satisfaction Index has the highest usability for forecasting a brand's economic future*. These authors clearly indicate that the NPS (discussed later in this chapter) has little or no predictive value in that case.

### Metric limitations

The above example helps you to understand why the CSI and the WSI are great for measuring satisfaction with services or more expensive durable goods, but not FMCG. It is hard to expect a yogurt buyer to evaluate several different attributes of a product, which usually does not cause deep deliberation. The fact that the buyer of yogurt is satisfied with the brand is perfectly demonstrated by repeat purchase or a high share of wallet (Chapter 5). On the other hand, using a car or staying in a holiday resort usually involves an informed evaluation on the part of the customer, who analyzes what he/she is and is not satisfied with.

## 4.5 Net Promoter Score

Several years ago, Fred Reichheld from Bain & Co. consultancy introduced a much simpler method of measuring customer satisfaction.

### Metric definition

*Net Promoter Score* is a simple measure of customer satisfaction obtained by answering just one question: 'How likely is it that you would recommend our company/product/service to a friend or colleague?', which is answered on an 11-point scale:

Very unlikely 0----1----2----3----4----5----6----7----8----9----10 Very likely

**Logic behind the metric**

Both the wording of a question and the scale on which answers are given have been chosen intentionally.

Why do we ask about satisfaction with a brand, referring to readiness to recommend it? To eliminate the influence of good manners and inborn politeness. To the question: 'Are you satisfied with us?', a polite person does not feel it fair to rate us below average (3 on a 5-point scale), unless the person has been treated very badly. In the vast majority of cases, a short scale (5-point) and referring to personal impressions and feelings cause high scores, which might be untrue regarding the actual brand experience. A customer who is not really impressed by the brand and who wants to be polite or would not feel comfortable telling the brand representative (waitress, hotel receptionist, etc.) that 'it was just so-so' would rather give a rating of 4, although fully aware that the brand does not deserve such a score. In the case of the 11-point scale, you can offend no one (at least you might think so) and at the same time demonstrate your incomplete satisfaction by giving a score of 6, 7 or even 8. Expanding the scale lets the customer say politely 'I was not delighted'.

Next, we do not ask 'were you satisfied?' but 'would you recommend us to friends or family?'. It is known that such a question puts brand evaluation in a different perspective. Not wanting to compromise the good relationships with loved ones, we will not recommend just any brand to them. The brand really has to delight customers in order to deserve such a recommendation. So, if your summer stay in a hotel was actually mediocre (not the worst food, so-so room and tolerable location), you can safely give a score of 6 or 7 which seemingly looks to be favourable for the brand, without putting you in an uncomfortable situation, but, on the other hand, not showing much enthusiasm for the brand.

**Metric calculation**

$$\begin{aligned}&\text{Net Promoter Score}\\&=\text{scores 9 and 10}\left(\text{promoters}\right)-\text{scores from 0 to 6}\left(\text{detractors}\right)\end{aligned} \tag{4.4}$$

The author of this metric defines people who give ratings of 9 or 10 as brand promoters. Those are the most satisfied buyers, who are not afraid of compromising their relationships with loved ones when they recommend a particular brand. Ratings of 7 or 8 are neutral (in fact, they should be interpreted as 'you know, this hotel was quite good but nothing special'). And the whole range from 0 to 6 (remember the natural tendency of the majority of people to some overrating of 'middle-of-the-road' brands) is treated as assessments of detractors, consumers not really satisfied with the brand.

### Metric interpretation

The NPS can be between –100 and +100, but most brands achieve NPS scores of between 10 and 16 (Gupta and Zeithaml 2006). On the netpromoter.com website, in the 'benchmarks' bookmark, you can find examples of industries and brands. For example, in 2016, the highest NPS (58) was for department stores, followed by tablets (47). Supermarkets and hotels had an average of 39, smartphones 38, and banks and airlines 35. Internet providers (2) and cable TV (7) were the lowest on the list.

### Case 1

*In 2020, smart home devices manufacturer FIBARO, mentioned earlier in this chapter, hired a market research agency to measure customer satisfaction (among others) globally, and one of the metrics used was the Net Promoter Score. The survey revealed that the percentage of neutral opinions in different parts of the world was pretty much the same (from 31% in Eastern Europe and North America to 43% in Western Europe). Major differences between regions were observed regarding the proportion of promoters vs. detractors. In some parts of the globe, the percentage of detractors was higher than promoters, resulting in a negative value for the NPS; in some parts (such as Southern Europe) as much as 38% of customers were promoters (twice as much as in Northern Europe or Australia); therefore, the NPS there was +17. Surprisingly, the percentage of promoters was higher in France, Italy and especially Spain, than in native Poland. In the case of hi-tech categories, such as smart home devices, customer experience with the brand covers many areas, not only product but also service related (e.g. installations and repairs). The inconsistent level of customer satisfaction, which was revealed by varying the values of the NPS, hints at possible problems with the standardization of the customer service provided by local distributors and installers.*

### Case 2

*The Crédit Agricole Group*[2] *has over 125 years of history in banking. The Crédit Agricole Group is present in 47 countries around the world. Currently, it is among the 10 largest banks in the world in terms of assets value and is also a leader in universal banking in France. The bank systematically measures customer satisfaction using the NPS metric (in internal documents it is titled the 'Customer Recommendation Index' but its calculation is the same as in the case of the NPS). Apart from the NPS metric, Crédit Agricole also looks for motivations behind customers' decisions regarding their choice of the bank and their evaluations of various areas of the bank's offerings. The methodology and research agency are the same in the case of each market, so the headquarters in Paris has a comparable outlook on customers' relative satisfaction in different markets. Of course, local competition in different countries varies and it might have an impact on customers' point of reference. Research in 2019 revealed that, for example, in Serbia, Crédit Agricole's NPS (53) was much higher than all local competitors – the NPS of bank no. 2 was just 43 and the average for retail banks was 33. Crédit Agricole is outnumbering the competition especially among customers aged 55 years plus – its NPS is 69 with its major competitor at just 49 (industry average in that age bracket is 36). In Poland, where some of its competitors have made huge progress in customer satisfaction (the leader of the 2019 ranking had improved its NPS from 15 to 57 in just three years; bank no. 2 from 17 to 42 in the same period), Crédit Agricole was no. 3 with an NPS of 33 (industry average was 26). It is interesting to note that affluent customers are relatively more demanding than the mass market – the industry's average NPS was 15 vs. 31 in the case of mass market customers (the same tendency can be observed in Serbia). The leader's NPS in Poland was 50 for affluent customers and 61 for the mass market and, in the case of Crédit Agricole, the scores were 23 and 36, respectively.*

## Metric limitations

When analyzing the NPS it should be remembered that the propensity to recommend the brand is conditioned by product category, which limits the possibility of comparing metrics with brands from other industries.

The problem is also with the arbitrary and not necessarily universal boundaries between detractors and neutral customers (why 6 and not 7?) and between them and promoters (why 8 and not 9?), as well as attributing equally destructive power to customers with a score of 0 and those with a score of 6[3] (Bendle and Bagga 2016).

Analysis by Keiningham et al. (2007), based on continuous research of 8,000 customers in three services (retail banking, retail trade, and internet providers), which included various satisfaction and loyalty metrics for a period of two years (and in the second year also customer retention and a brand's share of wallet), states unequivocally that treating the NPS as a good predictor of future purchasing behaviour (loyalty) is incorrect. In the opinion of those authors, the current tendency for managers to rely on the NPS alone to explain and predict consumer behaviour is wrong.

Apparently, the NPS fails to predict future sales, which only confirms the critical opinions about the NPS expressed in some publications (Sharp 2008). The NPS is not a metric whose high value would guarantee a safe future for the brand. In 2016, Nordstrom department stores had the highest NPS and three years later they struggled (operating profits at the level of half that of 2011) with Amazon which achieved a much lower NPS in 2016 (Mahashwari and Corkery 2019).

In addition, consultants emphasize the fact that the NPS completely ignores the experience of the service personnel, and ultimately the level of service delivered depends on them (Egol 2019).

## Recommendations for brand managers

1. Always analyze the Customer Satisfaction Index or the Weighted Satisfaction Index together with the distribution of answers. Check the percentages of extreme notes ('1' and '5' on a 5-point scale). In the case of a relatively (compared with rival brands) high percentage of '1' ratings, try to analyze not only the reasons for this but also which segment of the market was least satisfied. If, at the same time, your brand has a huge percentage of satisfied customers, maybe you target communication too broadly.

2. Even apparently high levels of the CSI (e.g. 3.60) should not reassure you that everything is OK when you have a large proportion of '3' and '4' scores (even if your research has not detected any dissatisfied customers). Remember that people are generally polite, yet in order to build a strong brand you should have passionate and delighted customers and not ones declaring that your brand is 'not that bad'. If your brand has a CSI of 3.60 and just 5% of '5' ratings, you most probably need to design customers' experience from scratch, and think of all those important customer touchpoints where you can really deliver a 'wow' experience.
3. The NPS should not be used alone without measuring partial satisfaction in all important areas of customer experience.
4. Do not use the NPS as a predictor of future sales.

### Questions

1. Why is measuring brand satisfaction complicated?
2. What categories of customers can we survey when measuring satisfaction?
3. What is the difference between the Customer Satisfaction Index and the Weighted Satisfaction Index?
4. What kind of analysis is possible when we ask not only about brand rating on various product attributes, but also their importance?
5. Why should we *not* use the 'top 2 boxes' formula for analyzing satisfaction?
6. What is the rationale behind asking 'How likely is it that you would *recommend* our company/product/service *to a friend or colleague*?'?
7. As a manager of a hotel chain, can you compare the NPS for your brand with leading airlines? Retailers? Why?

## Notes

1 All information regarding this case has been delivered by Anna Adrian, former CMO of FIBARO.

2 All information regarding this case has been delivered by Jedrzej Marciniak, head of marketing and vice president of Crédit Agricole Polska.

3 A good example of this problem might be the case (taken from Crédit Agricole's report) of two Serbian banks with nearly the same percentage of detractors (18% and 19%). Yet, one bank had just 9% of '5' or '6' ratings and 5% of '0' ratings. The other bank had 15% of '5' or '6' ratings and just 3% of '0' ratings. The methodology of the NPS calculation does not discriminate between brands with a majority of '6' ratings and those with a high percentage of '0' ratings, even though the difference in customer satisfaction is obvious.

## Literature

Ariely D., 2009, *Predictably Irrational: The Hidden Forces That Shape Our Decisions*, Harper Perennial, New York.

Bendle N.T., Bagga Ch.K., 2016, The Metrics That Marketers Muddle, *MIT Sloan Management Review*, Spring, pp. 73–81.

Bendle N.T., Farris P.W., Pfeifer Ph.E., Reibstein D.J., 2015, *Marketing Metrics: The Manager's Guide to Measuring Marketing Performance*, Pearson Education, Upper Saddle River.

East R., Wright M., Vanhuele M., 2008, *Consumer Behaviour: Applications in Marketing*, SAGE, Los Angeles.

Egol M., 2019, Three Reasons Net Promoter Score Is Past its Prime, *Strategy+Business*, 22 May, www. strategy-business.com/blog/Why-Net-Promoter-Score-is-past-its-prime?gko=dc66a [access: 29.09.2020].

Gupta S., Zeithaml V., 2006, Customer Metrics and Their Impact on Financial Performance, *Marketing Science*, 25(6), pp. 718–739, doi: 10.1287/mksc.1060.0221.

Keiningham T.L., Cooil B., Aksoy L., Andreassen T.W., Weiner J., 2007, The Value of Different Customer Satisfaction and Loyalty Metrics in Predicting Customer Retention, Recommendation, and Share-of-Wallet, *Managing Service Quality*, 17(4), pp. 361–384, doi: 10.1108/09604520710760526.

Maheshwari S., Corkery M., 2019, Chasing Amazon, Retailers Are in a Never-Ending Arms Race, *New York Times*, 26 November.

Morgan N.A., Rego L.L., 2006, The Value of Different Customer Satisfaction and Loyalty Metrics in Predicting Business Performance, *Marketing Science*, 25(5), pp. 426–439, doi: 10.1287/mksc.1050.0180.

netpromoter.com.

www.reviewtrackers.com/reports/online-reviews-survey/ [access: 13.10.2020].

Sharp B., 2008, Net Promoter Score Fails the Test – Market Research Buyers Beware, *Marketing Research*, Winter, pp. 28–30.

Stasiuk K., Maison D., 2014, *Psychologia Konsumenta*, PWN, Warszawa.

# 5

# MEASURING CUSTOMER RETENTION AND LOYALTY

**Learning objectives:**

After reading this chapter you should

- appreciate the importance of the repeat purchase in the case of new brands;
- understand the concept and recognize the limitations of customer loyalty;
- be familiar with the concept of the repertoire of brands and its impact on analyzing brand loyalty;
- be familiar with five metrics analyzing customer retention and loyalty: Customer Loyalty Ratio (CLR), repeat purchase rate, retention rate, share of wallet (SOW) and sole brand users;
- be able to calculate all of the above metrics;
- be aware of relatively small differences between share of wallet for competing brands and understand the reasons behind them.

Marketers from Procter & Gamble are credited with saying that there are only two important moments of truth: the first purchase and ... the second purchase. Many marketing activities are targeted primarily at increasing the trial rate and penetration. But next to so-called 'acquisition marketing', brand owners should undertake (some textbooks even suggest that managers should focus on) activities within so-called 'retention marketing', aimed at encouraging customers already acquired to stay with the brand.

## 5.1 Repeat purchase rate

The simplest way to investigate whether a new brand has managed to retain customers after a trial purchase is by analyzing the repurchase, or repeat purchase rate, which is clear proof of satisfaction with all branded touchpoints. Subsequent purchases confirm that the customer has accepted the brand.

DOI: 10.4324/9781003167235-5

### Metric definition

*Repeat purchase rate* is the percentage of brand buyers from the previous period of time who repeat their purchase nowadays.

### Metric calculation

$$\text{Repeat purchase rate} = 100 \star \text{number of brand buyers who repeat their purchase in the period } t : \text{number of brand buyers in the period } t-1 \quad (5.1)$$

or

$$\text{Repeat purchase rate} = 100 * \text{number of brand buyers who repeat their purchase in the period } t : \text{number of category buyers} \quad (5.2)$$

Repeat purchase, as calculated in Formula 5.2, is always lower than in the case of Formula 5.1. In both formulas, the numerator is the same but the denominator is larger in Formula 5.2.

The source of the data for calculating the repeat purchase rate should be surveys or consumer panels, which give more reliable estimates. In the case of brands competing in low-involvement categories (low: price, risk, level of search activity, remorse in the case of unsatisfactory delivery of benefits promised by the brand), some respondents in a survey might simply forget either the brand name or the time frame of the brand purchase; therefore, consumer panels are a much better option.

### Case

*Four months after its launch in the United Arab Emirates market, 'Rainbow for Coffee' whitener achieved a trial of 29% and a repeat purchase rate of 17% (among all category buyers) (Effie Awards 2019).*

### Repeat purchase rate in the case of infrequently purchased goods

Repeat purchase can also be analyzed for infrequently purchased goods (such as cars), where even an annual time horizon is too short, and the intervals between subsequent purchases for different buyers may differ significantly. Thus, in Formula 5.1 the period of a year cannot be replaced by another fixed time interval. Therefore, repeat purchase should be calculated as follows:

$$\text{Repeat purchase in the case of infrequently purchased goods} = 100 \star \text{number of brand buyers in purchase episode } n : \text{number of brand buyers in purchase episode } n-1 \quad (5.3)$$

Thus, calculated metrics inform what percentage of brand buyers repeat their previous choice. Two-thirds of buyers of leading car brands repeat their previous brand choice (Gorzelany 2016), and in the case of leading smartphone brands, it is nearly 70% (Moon 2019). Those values can be treated as benchmarks for those categories. Of course, other products require their own benchmark as a basis for comparisons.

**Metric interpretation**

The success of a new brand, revealed in a high percentage of repeat purchases, may result from

1. lack of alternatives (e.g. a newly established petrol station is the only one in a small village);
2. positive experiences with the brand and the desire to minimize purchasing effort that results in a habit (frequently purchased goods);
3. strongly felt risk in the case of a brand change (applies particularly to services); after finding an acceptable service provider it does not make sense to take the risk of searching for a new one that might be just a little bit better;
4. the fact that an adopted brand is cheaper (after taking into account the price and additional benefits offered);
5. barriers prohibiting brand change (contracts signed, concessions and privileges obtained, etc.).

At the initial stage of launching a new brand, the repeat purchase rate is usually lower (e.g. 60%), and only then does it begin to *increase* (e.g. to 80%), because customers' preferences tend to stabilize. That is why, after a few quarters following a brand's launch, *a systematic analysis of the repeat purchase rate will not reveal much* – those customers who liked a brand the least, abandoned it after the first purchase; after the second purchase, the brand might be dropped by customers who were still hesitant, not fully convinced by its attributes. With each succeeding purchase, the probability that a brand becomes part of the repertoire (see also Sections 2.1.1 and 5.2) and is purchased fairly regularly is growing. Only a small percentage of yogurt buyers who have purchased brand X regularly in the last half-year are not going to continue buying it this month. Of course, it is possible that the brand is abandoned due to changes in diet, the search for healthier or cheaper alternatives to the previously bought brand, or because of scandals surrounding the brand owner, quality problems or unethical practices that the consumer does not tolerate. Yet, the overwhelming majority of brand buyers are going to stay with the brand, from a tendency for routine behaviour, which allows them to concentrate on more interesting things in life than choosing the right brand of yogurt.

In light of the above-mentioned mechanisms, when a new brand registers a *decrease* in repeat purchase rates between the second and third quarter following its launch, this is a clear signal of the problems awaiting it in the future (Singh and Wright 2016).

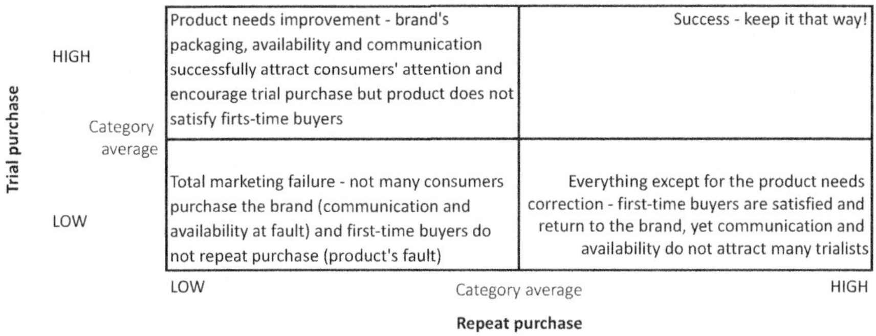


**FIGURE 5.1** Analysis of a new brand's trial and repeat purchase rates.

In the case of brands just entering the market, an analysis of the repeat purchase rate together with the trial rate (see Section 3.2.1) allows an assessment of the effectiveness of its marketing (see Figure 5.1).

**Metric limitations**

If we study a short period of time (e.g. a month), it may turn out that only a small percentage of the brand buyers from the previous month repeat the brand purchase in the following month. This is not because of the unattractiveness of the brand ('lost customer'), but because of the natural tendency for some customers to purchase a given product category relatively rarely (e.g. once a quarter). This means that even in the case of frequently purchased goods, it is better to analyze the repeat purchase rate for longer periods (half-year, year) than for shorter ones.

## 5.2 Problems with measuring brand loyalty

Loyalty is assigned exceptional importance in marketing textbooks. Without it, a brand would have no chance of success, so marketers should get it at all costs. Loyalty (implicitly, purchasing just one brand in a category[1]) is described as a desirable condition for every brand. Is this really feasible? Let us analyze problems with the measurement of customers' behaviour returning to a brand.

If we add the penetration rates (see Section 3.2.2) of all brands in the majority of categories, the sum significantly exceeds 100%, usually achieving levels of 200% or even 300%. This is due to the fact that *no market is composed of 100% loyal customers*, but rather those who buy simultaneously two, three and sometimes even more brands in a category, especially fast-moving consumer goods (FMCG). An analysis by Bain & Co. (2013) indicates that the average buyer simultaneously purchases somewhere between two (1.9) brands of detergents and up to six (5.6) brands of chocolate. In 2018, Nielsen estimated that beer drinkers in the UK consumed on average 2.84 brands, while in Ireland it was just 2.4 (Stoney and Mawdsley 2020). Usually, customers purchase a so-called *repertoire of brands* (Ehrenberg 1998). The reasons for having a repertoire of brands can be varied (East et al. 2008): appreciating variety, buying the cheapest brand at a given moment, unavailability of a preferred brand in the store, not remembering the brand you bought recently and sometimes pure convenience.[2]

The tendency to repetitively purchase selected, already-known brands is motivated by the desire to simplify shopping (to reduce not only the consideration time and the effort associated with it, but also the risk of buying an unknown brand).

Citing many categories of products and services, Schwartz (2004) explains why having too broad a choice within a category paradoxically makes many shoppers unhappy. Sharp (2017) claims that consumers' tendency to simplify shopping is *natural*, and is not the result of the marketing activities of brand owners. In his view, consumers usually show biased, non-random, repetitive choices in their shopping, limiting purchases to the repertoire of accepted, favourite brands.[3] An explanation of this phenomenon may be research that dates back to the early 1960s, in which it was proved that having the choice of an identical product (bread in one case; beer in another), but marked with different letters or placed differently on the shelves, most buyers whose purchases had been observed for a period of several days, had developed some *routine* behaviour (Sharp 2017). They chose either the product with the same letter or the product placed in the same corner of the shelf. We should emphasize once again, that in order to create that habit, no special actions were needed to differentiate brands from competitors, other than random letters and shelf placements.

Consequently, Sharp (2017) talks about '*prosaic*' loyalty, which is the opposite of the passionate loyalty that marketing textbooks usually praise. Development of the habit is a rational strategy for the shopper, allowing him/her to reduce the level of risk associated with making purchases while saving valuable time.[4]

On the other hand, one might counterargue that consumers are naturally attracted to new, unknown brands as our mind is aroused by everything that is new. True, but according to the neuroscientist Vetulani, the desire to experience the new is confronted with the imprinted fear of what is unknown (Vetulani and Mazurek 2015). In fact, routine in many cases takes over from that curiosity.

Lastly, we should beware of misinterpreting customer behaviour, whose buying pattern looks like XXXZZZ, as switching brand X to brand Z (Sharp et al. 2012). In fact, both may be his/her repertoire of brands, and both are equally liked and purchased with 50% probability. How can we explain that a purchase pattern that looks like XXXZZZ is a reflection of a brand repertoire? Why not the pattern XZXZXZ, which seems to reflect loyalty shared by two brands in an 'expected' way?

If you look again at the pattern above, you might notice that if we switch brands in the case of just two purchase occasions, the second and the fifth (Z instead of X in the case of the second purchase and X instead of Z in the case of the fifth purchase), we would get an XZXZXZ purchase pattern, that presumably perfectly fits our perception of divided loyalty. Can we then reasonably raise the problem that the customer has switched one brand for another for good, just because on one-third of purchase occasions he/she does not buy the brand we might expect? There are dozens of reasons for such deviations: price promotions, out of stock, a short stay from a niece who prefers Z over X, sampling, seeing an ad close to the shopping trip and many, many others. Yet still, that particular customer has *not* switched from X to Z but is equally predisposed to purchase either of them.

Getting back to metrics, if we agree that loyalty means the unconstrained purchase of only one brand in a category, then there is just one way to measure it, which is sole brand users (see Section 5.3). We will soon learn that in FMCG categories, the percentages of sole brand users are usually quite small. On the other hand, in some categories (such as insurance policies), customers have a natural tendency to use one brand at a time. And that might imply that the retention marketing of insurance and banking brands is extremely effective (almost all of them have extremely high levels of sole brand users), which is not true. Next are categories that rely on a subscription model (telecommunication companies, internet and cable TV providers, magazine publishers, some medical services, etc.), where the only metric to measure 'loyalty' is the retention rate (covered in Section 5.4). If we accept that in many categories it is natural for customers to have a repertoire of brands, then only share of wallet (see Section 5.5) is the right metric to measure a brand's position relative to its competitors. The Customer Loyalty Ratio is the last metric and this will be covered in Section 5.6. Although its name suggests otherwise, in reality it measures purchase intentions (the CLR is not that different from the metric covered in Section 2.4), and not true loyalty.

If we believe in loyalty as an amalgam of positive brand attitudes and a tendency to purchase the brand, there are better options to measure it than the Customer Loyalty Ratio. For example, Keller (2013) suggests that loyalty should be measured by a battery of statements: 'I consider myself loyal to this brand'; 'I buy this brand whenever I can'; 'I buy as much of this brand as I can'; 'I feel this is the only brand of this product I need'; 'This is the one brand I would prefer to buy/use'; 'If this brand were not available, it would make little difference to me if I had to use another brand'; 'I would go out of my way to use this brand'. By agreeing with these statements, the respondent substantiates his/her loyalty, if by loyalty we understand mainly the affective relationship with the brand. Please note that this battery of questions allows you to diagnose loyalty at a much deeper level, compared with a declaration of intention to purchase (Customer Loyalty Ratio).

## 5.3 Sole brand users

The metric closest to the common understanding of loyalty is referred to as *sole brand users*, which measures not declarations but actual behaviour.

### Metric definition

Sole brand users are those buyers who are 100% loyal to one brand within a product category.

### Metric calculation

$$\text{Sole brand users} = 100 * \text{customers buying only brand X} : \text{all brand X buyers} \tag{5.4}$$

### Metric interpretation

Having a relatively high percentage of sole brand users may be explained either by a high level of satisfaction and loyalty, or limited access to other brands. In other words, a high percentage of sole brand users can result either from faithful attachment to the brand 'for good and for bad' (loyalty), the lack of alternatives (the only gas station in a small town) or a natural tendency of customers to use only one brand at a time in a category. A good example is insurance policies or banking services – according to research by Sharp et al. (2002), in many cases, banks issuing credit cards have at least 50% (sometimes even 80% or more) sole brand users. Also, share of wallet scores in those cases tend to be higher than those suggested in Section 5.5.

The percentage of sole brand users (as well as a brand's share of wallet) tends to decrease as the analysis period extends because the longer the time period taken into account, the greater the likelihood that the consumer may have an opportunity to break his/her loyalty to the brand. In a short period of time, 'sole usage' may be explained by the fact that many consumers have just purchased one unit of a product.

Last but not least, market leaders usually have a higher (even twice as many) percentage of sole brand users than smaller brands,[5] although there are some exceptions. One of them is private labels, with relatively smaller market shares but having a disproportionately high percentage of sole users.

### Metric limitations

There are a few important things regarding that metric.

First of all, in the case of brands in FMCG categories, just *half* of their buyers over a period of a year might be those who *purchase just one or two packages*. As Ehrenberg's 'law of buying frequencies' demonstrates, the distribution of product purchase frequencies is left-skewed – each product has a majority of one-time (occasional) buyers and a very small percentage of heavy buyers (Sharp 2017). Those several percent of one-time buyers are, by definition, 'sole brand users', which does not reflect the true nature of their relation to the brand.

Secondly, research by Ehrenberg and Goodhardt (2002) proves that brands with large and small market shares differ slightly in terms of customer loyalty. As Sharp (2017) claims, every brand has its share of loyal customers, which is usually pretty similar to other brands in the category. Analyzing the percentage of sole brand buyers in four categories of FMCG (deodorants, breakfast cereals, yogurts and painkillers; Sharp 2017), it can be seen that, *on average, only every ninth buyer is 100% loyal to one brand*. Significantly more (2.5 times) sole brand users have painkillers, and much less (just 2%–7%), brands of yogurt and cereals. This is associated not so much (as one might think) with the level of purchasing risk, but with the average number of product purchases per year. Yogurt and cereals are bought about five to six times more often than painkillers. What's more, among buyers of painkillers, there is a considerable percentage of one-off shoppers, who are automatically counted as 100% loyal.

Last but not least, according to many authors (Sharp 2017; Singh and Uncles 2016; Sharp et al. 2002), sole brand users are generally light category buyers. Research indicates that they often purchase two to three times less of a product than the average category buyer (Ehrenberg et al. 2004). It is typical for heavy category users to have many opportunities to switch (even if just once) the most frequently bought brand, and then they are no longer 100% loyal.

## 5.4 Retention rate

### Metric definition

*Retention rate* is the percentage of customers who may have left (contract has ended), yet have decided to stay with the brand. Note that it is *not* the ratio of brand buyers at the beginning of a given period (e.g. year) to the number of customers at the beginning of the previous period (year), as some authors (e.g. Davis 2018) suggest. In such a case, next to customers retained by a brand, new customers acquired during a year are also included, and in effect we would be measuring the effectiveness not only of retention but also of acquisition activities.

### Metric calculation

$$\text{Retention rate} = 100 * \text{customers staying with the brand} : \text{customers with a contract ending} \quad (5.5)$$

Numbers are readily available for brands operating on a subscription or contract basis. Yet, the brand owner has to decide on a definition of a customer (if a customer decides to cancel his/her contract with a telecom, and at the same time his/her family resolves to have a mobile plan for all members of the family, how should the telecom count that user?) and take into account the many services that the same brand may offer (one may have decided to cancel a credit card account, yet retain a current account at the same bank – is this customer a retained customer or not?). How you define 'a customer' depends on the purpose of the measurement and there is no universal approach to it (Bendle et al. 2016).

### Metric interpretation

The retention rate applies to products/services purchased on a subscription basis or under long-term contracts (telecommunications, magazine subscription, insurance, banking services, cable TV, internet providers). It explores the effectiveness of retaining customers whose contract with the brand has ended. Research shows that brands usually manage to retain 85% of their acquired customers for a year; in the case of service brands where customers have a subscription contract, the retention rate ranges from *80% to 96%* (East et al. 2008).

It should be emphasized that not all lost customers have left the brand because of the brand owner's fault. Some have stopped using the product altogether (they have paid off their mortgage and do not need a new one), some have changed their address and a brand is unavailable in the new location, while some may have died. Therefore, it is unreasonable to set a target of keeping 100% customers because it is simply impossible to achieve. It would be a mistake to focus solely on retaining customers (often at all cost) while underestimating actions to increase brand penetration.

**Case**

(1) *Art Fund, a British charity established in 1903, is dedicated to the purpose of saving works of art. It has been a major source of funding for hundreds of museums and galleries in the United Kingdom. Art Fund relies primarily on membership with yearly subscriptions and the charity manages to run quite effectively – with the exception of 2008 (the global financial crisis). For the whole period of 2006–2015, Art Fund managed to retain at least 83.6% (up to 89.2%) of its members each year. The members pay for a National Art Pass, which allows them free or discounted entry to selected museums, galleries, castles and historic houses all over Britain (Smith 2016).*

(2) *The Automobile Association's (AA) membership retention rate increased in 2017 to nearly 83%. McKinsey has estimated the highest potential rate at 86%, due to members dying or moving to joint cover (after marriage) (Sussman 2018).*

## Metric limitations

After analyzing several markets, Riebe et al. (2014) claim that acquisition explains roughly twice the changes in market share in comparison to defection.[6] Therefore, concentrating on retention/defection metrics tells less than half the story.

A collection of case studies prepared for the Effectiveness Awards demonstrates that in the majority of cases, marketing campaigns targeted at loyalty underperform on almost every metric. Paradoxically, even when they work, they increase penetration rather than loyalty! A good example might be the $O_2$ mobile carrier campaign from 2006. It was aimed at reducing churn (see note 6) and increasing loyalty by offering rewards for it. The case study details an admirable reduction in churn, yet around two-thirds of the brand's market share growth came from acquiring new customers and only one-third from reducing churn (Binet and Field 2007). In increasing market share, activities aimed at penetration growth are much more effective than loyalty based (for more on this, see Section 7.2.1). For the majority of brand managers, it is much more important and feasible to constantly acquire new buyers (increase penetration) than to try and retain as many of them as possible.

Brands that lose market share and those that grow organically tend to lose some of their customers. It is therefore wise to compare the retention/defection rate of an examined brand to competitors or averages in the industry, and react only when it is at a *considerably* lower/higher level.

**Other applications of the metric**

Knowing the current market share of a brand and planning specific marketing activities that can affect both the defection and acquisition rates (percentage of potential customers acquired by a brand's marketing activities), it is easy to calculate what the brand's market share will be after a period of $n$ years (note: both the acquisition and defection rates should be in decimal terms):

$$\begin{aligned}&\text{Brand market share in year } n\\&= \text{initial market share}\\&\star \left[1+\begin{pmatrix}\text{customer acquisition rate as a result of marketing activity}\\ - \text{defection rate after marketing activity}\end{pmatrix} + (\text{initial acquisition rate} - \text{initial defection rate})\right]^n\end{aligned} \tag{5.6}$$

where

$n$ is the number of years.

For example, if brand X had an initial market share of 5%, acquiring 10% new customers every year and losing 9%, and as a result of a planned marketing activity the acquisition rate increased to 12% (increase by 20%) and the defection rate decreased to 6% per annum (one-third lower than it was before), then in the third year brand X would have a market share of $5 \star (1 + 0.06 + 0.01)^3 = 6.12\%$.

## 5.5 Brand's share of wallet

**Metric definition**

*Share of wallet* (also called share of requirements) is the share of category purchases that brand buyers dedicate to a given brand.

**Metric calculation**

Share of wallet is calculated (preferably on the basis of consumer panels) as follows:

$$\begin{aligned}\text{Share of wallet} &= 100 \star \text{brand purchases (volume/value)}:\\&\quad \text{product purchases made by brand buyers (volume/value)}\end{aligned} \tag{5.7}$$

Share of wallet can also be estimated as (see Formula 7.2)

$$\text{Share of wallet} = 100 \star \text{market share} : (\text{penetration rate} \star \text{heavy usage index})^{7} \quad (5.8)$$

**Alternative way to calculate the metric**

Consultants at Ipsos (Keiningham et al. 2011) suggest a simple formula to calculate the SOW:

$$\text{Share of wallet} = \left[\frac{1 - \text{rank of a brand in the repertoire/consideration set} :}{\left(\text{number of brands in the repertoire/consideration set} + 1\right)}\right] \star \left(2 : \text{number of brands in the repertoire/consideration set}\right) \quad (5.9)$$

In order to estimate the SOW, you need to conduct a survey among brand users asking them two questions: how many brands in the category they purchase (number of brands in the repertoire might also be taken from adding up the penetration rates of all brands in the category and dividing the sum by 100) or consider purchasing? and what is the rank of the given brand among them? Comparing the real values of share of wallet with scores calculated according to Formula 5.9, the researchers achieved over 90% correlation. Table 5.1 shows the SOW scores for some selected values.

A few interesting regularities can be observed in Table 5.1.

Let us start with the observation that differences in the SOW between pairs of succeeding brands (between brand no. 1 and 2 vs. between brand no. 2 and 3 vs. between brand no. 3 and 4, etc.), for a given number of brands in the repertoire, are identical[8]. Next, we can see that the more brands in the repertoire, the lower the leader's relative (compared with brand no. 2) share of wallet. When

**TABLE 5.1** Estimated share of wallet according to the number of brands in a repertoire (or consideration set) and brand's rank

| *Brand's rank* | *Number of brands in the repertoire or consideration set* | | | | | | |
|---|---|---|---|---|---|---|---|
| | *2 (%)* | *2.5 (%)* | *3 (%)* | *3.5 (%)* | *4 (%)* | *4.5 (%)* | *5 (%)* |
| 1 | 67 | 57 | 50 | 44 | 40 | 36 | 33 |
| 1.5 | 50 | 46 | 42 | 38 | 35 | 32 | 30 |
| 2 | 33 | 34 | 33 | 32 | 30 | 28 | 27 |
| 2.5 | | 23 | 25 | 25 | 25 | 24 | 23 |
| 3 | | | 17 | 19 | 20 | 20 | 20 |
| 3.5 | | | | 13 | 15 | 16 | 17 |
| 4 | | | | | 10 | 12 | 13 |
| 4.5 | | | | | | 8 | 10 |
| 5 | | | | | | | 7 |

the repertoire of brands expands, brand no. 1 loses its share of wallet faster than brand no. 2, and brand no 2 loses its share of wallet faster than brand no. 3 and so forth. At the same time, the more brands in the repertoire, the higher the ratio of share of wallet of brand no. 1 and of the last brand. In fact, that ratio equals the number of brands in the repertoire.[9]

We can conclude that only from the perspective of the leader, the suggestion to limit the repertoire of brands is sensible. The lower the number of brands in a repertoire, the higher (significantly) its share of wallet. If you are the owner of the brand ranked third in the repertoire, and the set of brands expands, it is even better for your brand's share of wallet! You have no incentive to make buyers more loyal to a few leading brands!

### Metric interpretation

One might call a brand's share of wallet a special case of 'market share' if, by a market, we mean all purchases by current brand buyers. The larger a brand's share of wallet, the more brand buyers are attached to it, so it is also a specific metric of customer loyalty (meant not so as much as exclusive purchases of the same brand, but rather a positive attitude towards it).

Share of wallet is used in many markets: FMCG, finance, tourism, entertainment, B2B. In the case of a new brand of frequently purchased goods (FMCG), we might observe the SOW stabilizing shortly after its launch. Brands that are going to have large market shares shortly after entering the market show an SOW at the level of market leaders. This proves not only customers' acceptance of a product, but also the whole shopping experience offered under the brand's name.

A brand's SOW decreases as the analyzed period is extended: the longer the time period taken into account, the greater the likelihood that customers will reach for other brands in a given category. A brand might have an SOW of 40% if a quarter of the year is analyzed; in the half-year period it may have an SOW of e.g. 30%; and over the year just 25%. The reasons for reaching for other brands can be trivial: occasional problems with availability, shopping in a store other than a regular one, which may be the result of a holiday trip and the like.

Share of wallet is very useful for determining the potential for increasing business generated by current brand customers. *The lower the level of actual SOW, the greater the potential for increasing it*, and vice versa: the more loyal to a brand its customers already are (higher value of share of wallet), the harder it is to increase it.[10] If a brand has an SOW of 50%, significantly increasing it is much more difficult than if a brand has an SOW of 10%.

### Case

*In 2015–2016, millennials accounted for ca. 35% of online apparel revenue in the United States. Among them, the share of wallet of leading apparel e-retailers was as follows: Amazon – 16.6%, Nordstrom – 8.1%, Old Navy – 5.1% and J. Crew – 4.2% (Stanton 2017).*

It should be emphasized that share of wallet scores for competing brands do not differ as much as their penetration rates do (Jones 1998). To explain why, let's decompose Formula 5.7 into prime factors:

$$\text{Share of wallet} = \left(\begin{array}{l}\text{number of brand purchases} \star \text{average number of brand packages} \\ \text{bought at a shopping trip} \star \text{brand packaging size}\end{array}\right) : \left(\begin{array}{l}\text{number of product purchases by average brand buyer} \\ \star \text{ average number of product packages bought} \\ \text{by brand buyers on a shopping trip} \star \text{average packaging size}\end{array}\right) \quad (5.10)$$

Usually, there are no big differences between brands in the number of packages purchased on each shopping trip. It would be quite strange if the average buyer of mustard X bought twice as many jars of it as the average buyer of mustard Y. What is more, the packaging sizes of competing brands are usually similar (consider milk, beer, washing powder and many other FMCG). When we decompose the SOW in volume terms, the only factor that differentiates brands is the *number of brand purchases* made by the average brand buyer over a period of a year.

Additionally, one should consider that, on an annual basis, the average number of packages purchased for any FMCG usually ranges from a few to 12 or so (Sharp 2017). That is why the SOW of the least frequently bought brand will never be lower than 10% or so! Remember that SOW relates to purchases made by brand buyers, and not all category buyers. Even if a passionate customer of a breakfast cereal brand purchases 20 packages a year, and buys that brand just once, its SOW is still 5%. On the other hand, there will be many more single-purchase cereal buyers (Jones and Slater 2003) for whom the SOW of brands is 100%. If we calculate the average SOW, the minimal value of it, under real market conditions, rarely falls below several *12%*.

Now, comparing the minimum SOW (say, just 10%) with the SOW for the market leaders of a given category (rarely exceeding 35%–40%; see Table 5.1), it turns out that the difference is much smaller (in practice rarely more than three times) than the difference in their penetration rates. In the case of penetration, brands just entering the market differ from market leaders dozen or even several dozen times (e.g. 40% penetration for the market leader vs. 1% for a newly launched brand).

## 5.6 Customer Loyalty Ratio

### Metric definition

*Customer Loyalty Ratio* is the percentage of brand buyers who declare that they are going to purchase the brand in the future.

### Metric calculation

The loyalty ratio is determined on the basis of a declaration in a survey of brand buyers regarding purchasing a brand in the future. Respondents use the scale: 'I will definitely buy this brand'; 'I would rather buy'; 'I would rather not buy'; 'I will certainly not buy'; 'it is difficult to say'. Then, we calculate the metrics as follows:

$$\text{Standard Loyalty Ratio} \\ = 100 * \text{declarations 'I will definitely buy' and 'I would rather buy'} \\ \left(\text{an examined brand}\right) : \text{all surveyed brand buyers} \tag{5.11}$$

or as

$$\text{Enhanced Loyalty Ratio} \\ = 100 \star \text{declarations I will definitely buy an examined brand'} : \\ \text{all surveyed brand buyers} \tag{5.12}$$

### Metric interpretation

The main difference between the Customer Loyalty Ratio and brand purchase intentions (see Section 2.3) is that the former metric relates to actual brand buyers and the latter to all category buyers.

As a rule, loyalty ratios calculated as above obtain relatively higher values in the case of high involvement (thus high risk) services such as banks and insurance, while significantly lower values for FMCG.

### Case

*The customer loyalty of iPhone users peaked in 2017 – according to BankMyCell (which collected data from over 38,000 iPhones users) – when it was at 92%. In 2019, it declined to 73% (McCarthy 2019). BankMyCell estimated Samsung's loyalty at 64% in the same year (Kozuch 2019).*

### Metric limitations

The Customer Loyalty Ratio cannot be diagnosed in the case of one-off products (a pop concert) or rarely purchased goods (e.g. an apartment).

### Recommendations for brand managers

1. When launching a new brand, one has to analyze not only its trial rate but also its repeat purchase rate, which is clear proof of satisfaction with all branded touchpoints. Both metrics should be used to analyze the effectiveness of a new brand's marketing.
2. You should be alarmed in the case of a decreasing repeat purchase rates between the second and third quarter following the launch of a new brand.

3. The Customer Loyalty Ratio is just a declaration of brand buyers. The real behaviour is measured only by 'share of wallet', 'sole brand users' or 'retention rate'. If you have the choice, it is always better to analyze share of wallet or retention rate than the Customer Loyalty Ratio.
4. In businesses operating on a contractual basis, you should be alarmed if a brand has a retention rate below 80%.
5. You should expect your brand's share of wallet to be in the range of 10%–50%, depending on the number of brands in the repertoire and the brand's rank in it. Higher values would suggest a stronger market position; lower values would suggest that your brand is purchased for special occasions, for variety or only when 'on sale'.
6. You should not focus all your marketing efforts on increasing share of wallet, but rather on building penetration.

## Questions

1. If the trial rate for a new brand is higher than the industry average, yet its repeat purchase rate is much lower, should we spend more on advertising or on product improvements?
2. Are sole brand users responsible for a substantial percentage of a brand's sales?
3. Do values of share of wallet differ more between market leaders and smaller brands than their penetrations rates?
4. Using Formula 5.8, calculate the share of wallet metric (for 2019) for three brands of beer: Lech Premium, Tyskie Gronie and Zubr. Base your calculations on the relevant data in Tables 1.5 and 7.1, making the assumption that heavy usage indices equal 1 in each case. Which of the brands has the most and which has the least loyal drinkers?
5. Is brand loyalty a result of exceptionally good marketing or something else?

## Notes

1 As such, it should be measured by just one metric: sole brand users (explained in Section 5.3).

2 Kantar analysis of Tesco shoppers in the UK shows that 70%–80% of shoppers of *every* retail chain in the UK, also shop at Tesco at least once in the course of a year (Clouder 2018). It looks as though having many locations (i.e. more convenient shopping) in many instances wins over 'loyalty'.

3 Sharp (2017) refers to Sorensen's analysis from 2009, showing that, every year, the average consumer purchases only a few hundred brands out of many thousands available in stores.

4 A Millward Brown Digital (2015) analysis shows that in the case of electronics, on deciding which brand to buy, consumers who are 100% loyal to a brand spend threefold less time than non-loyal consumers. The stage of actively searching for information is, in this case, 5.5 times shorter. No doubt being loyal has an impact on how we buy – it reduces the time spent on shopping.

5 For example, leaders of the Polish market in frozen pizza and fruit tea have twice as many sole brand buyers than brand no. 6 in those categories.

6 Defection rate (churn) = 100% – retention rate.
7 The heavy usage index can be omitted as it is usually close to 1 (see Section 7.2).
8 Because of the rounding, in some cases the differences are one percentage point larger.
9 In reality, it never happens that all the respondents in a survey declare the same ranking for brands, so the leader will never have the rank of 1 but rather 1.5 and the last brand in the repertoire of $n$ brands will never have a rank of $n$ but rather something in between $n - 1$ and $n$. Therefore, in the case of (let's say) five brands in a repertoire, the difference in the share of wallet between the leader and the last brand is not 5 (in Table 5.1 the values of the SOW are rounded; in the case of a brand ranked first, its SOW is exactly 33.3% and the SOW for a brand ranked fifth is 6.66%, so the ratio equals 5), but rather 3 (30% SOW for the brand ranked 1.5 vs. 10% SOW for the brand ranked 4.5).
10 Of course, the brand owner may take action to increase the consumption of the product, and this is often effective, yet it does not necessarily mean increasing the brand's SOW.

## Literature


Bendle N.T., Farris P.W., Pfeifer Ph.E., Reibstein D.J., 2016, *Marketing Metrics: The Manager's Guide to Measuring Marketing Performance*, Third Edition, Pearson Education, Upper Saddle River.

Binet L., Field P., 2007, *Marketing in the Era of Accountability: Identifying the Marketing Practices and Metrics That Truly Increase Profitability*, World Advertising Research Center, Henley-on-Thames.

Clouder J., 2018, How Lidl Grew a Lot, in: *Advertising Works 24: Proving the Payback on Marketing Investment*, ed. N. Godber, Institute of Practitioners in Advertising + WARC, London, pp. 227–252.

Davis J.A., 2018, *Measuring Marketing – The 100+ Essential Metrics Every Marketer Needs*, Third Edition, Walter de Gruyter Inc, Boston.

East R., Wright M., Vanhuele M., 2008, *Consumer Behaviour: Applications in Marketing*, SAGE, Los Angeles.

Effie Awards, 2019, www.effie.org/case_database/case/MN_2019_099.

Ehrenberg A.S.C., 1998, Repetitive Advertising and the Consumer, in: *How Advertising Works: The Role of Research*, ed. J.Ph. Jones, SAGE, Thousand Oaks, pp. 63–81.

Ehrenberg A.S.C., Goodhardt G., 2002, Double Jeopardy Revisited, Again, *Marketing Research*, 14(1), p. 40, doi: 10.1177/002224299005400307.

Ehrenberg A.S.C., Uncles M.D., Goodhardt G., 2004, Understanding Brand Performance Measures: Using Dirichlet Benchmarks, *Journal of Business Research*, 57(12), pp. 1307–1325, doi: 10.1016/j.jbusres.2002.11.001.

Gorzelany J., 2016, Cars and Crossovers Drivers Would Buy or Lease Again, *Forbes*, 19 January.

Jones J.Ph., 1998, Penetration, Brand Loyalty, and the Penetration Supercharge, in: *How Advertising Works: The Role of Research*, ed. J.Ph. Jones, SAGE, Thousand Oaks, pp. 57–62.

Jones J.Ph., Slater J.S., 2003, *What's In a Name ? Advertising and the Concept of Brands*, M.E. Sharpe, Armonk.

Keiningham T.L., Aksoy L., Buoye A., Cooil B., 2011, Customer Loyalty Isn't Enough. Grow Your Share of Wallet, *Harvard Business Review*, October, pp. 29–31.

Keller K.L., 2013, *Strategic Brand Management: Building, Measuring, and Managing Brand Equity. Global Edition*, Pearson, Harlow.

Kozuch K., 2019, Samsung Leads the Way for Android Phone Brand Loyalty, *Tom's Guide*, 31 July, www.tomsguide.com/news/samsung-leads-the-way-for-android-phone-brand-loyalty-report [access: 9.01.2021].

Mc Carthy N., 2019, Loyalty Is Waning Among iPhone Users, *Forbes*, 22 July.

Millward Brown, 2015, *Demystifying the Consumer Journey: Establishing a Consumer-Centric Marketing Strategy*, Millward Brown Digital.

Moon M., 2019, Americans Are Waiting Three Years to Replace Their Phones, Study Finds, *Endgadget*, 23 August www.engadget.com/2019-08-23-us-phone-upgrade-strategy-analytics.html? [access: 9.11.2020].

Riebe E., Wright M., Stern Ph., Sharp B., 2014, How to Grow a Brand: Retain or Acquire Customers?, *Journal of Business Research*, 67, pp. 990–997, doi: 10.1016/j.jbusres.2013.08.005.

Schwartz B., 2004, *The Paradox of Choice – Why More Is Less; How the Culture of Abundance Robs Us of Satisfaction*, Harper Collins, New York.

Sharp B., 2017, *Marketing: Theory, Evidence, Practice*, Second Edition, Oxford University Press, Sydney.

Sharp B, Wright M., Goodhardt G., 2002, Purchase Loyalty Is Polarised into Either Repertoire or Subscription Patterns, *Australasian Marketing Journal*, 10(3), pp. 7–20, doi: 10.1016/S1441-3582(02)70155-9.

Sharp B., Wright M., Dawes J., Driesener C., Meyer-Waarden L., Stocchi L., Stern Ph., 2012, It's a Dirichlet World: Modelling Individuals' Loyalties Reveals How Brands Compete, Grow, and Decline, *Journal of Advertising Research*, June, pp. 203–213, doi: 10.2501/JAR-52-2-203-213.

Singh J., Uncles M., 2016, Measuring the Market Performance of Brands: Applications in Brand Management, in: *The Routledge Companion to Contemporary Brand Management*, ed. F. Dall'Olmo Riley, J. Singh, Ch. Blankson, Routledge, London, pp. 13–31.

Singh J., Wright M., 2016, New Brands: Performance and Measurement, in: *The Routledge Companion to Contemporary Brand Management*, ed. F. Dall'Olmo Riley, J. Singh, Ch. Blankson, Routledge, London, pp. 186–197.

Smith J., 2016, Art. Fund: The Art of Framing, in: *Advertising Works 23: Proving the Payback on Marketing Investment*, ed. B. Angear, Institute of Practitioners in Advertising + WARC, London, pp. 109–138.

Stanton T., 2017, ASOS Wins the Hearts and Wallets of Millennials Online, *The BRIEF Blog*, 23 February, www.rakutenintelligence.com/blog/2017/asos-wins-hearts-wallets-millennials-online [access: 7.01.2021].

Stoney L., Mawdsley C., 2020, Guinness 'Made of More' 2012–2019: Consistency x Creativity, in: *Advertising Works 25: Proving the Payback on Marketing Investment*, ed. S. Unerman, Institute of Practitioners in Advertising + WARC by Ascential, London, pp. 147–196.

Sussman T., 2018, The AA: From Spark-Plugs to Singalongs, in: *Advertising Works 24: Proving the Payback on Marketing Investment*, ed. N. Godber, Institute of Practitioners in Advertising + WARC, London, pp. 305–348.

Vetulani J., Mazurek M., 2015, *Bez Ograniczen – Jak rzadzi nami mozg*, PWN, Warszawa.

Webster R., Dhiri S., Frame T., Dorsett Ph., 2013, *Learning How to Change with UK Shoppers*, "Bain and Co Report", 25 March, www.bain.com/insights/learning-how-to-change-with-uk-shoppers/ [access: 15.12.2020]

# 6

# MEASURING BRAND ADVOCACY

**Learning objectives:**

After reading this chapter you should

- understand the role of social media in consumer purchase decisions and recognize the limitations of its measurement;
- be familiar with two specific metrics analyzing brand advocacy: Brand Advocacy Index (BAI) and Brand Advocacy Ratio (BAR);
- be able to calculate both of these metrics.

## 6.1 Social media in consumer decisions and the difficulties with measurement

When customers are satisfied, and maybe even loyal users of a brand, its owner might expect that they start recommending the brand to others, whether in face-to-face conversations, on internet forums or on social media. There seems to be little doubt as to the importance of social media in the case of the B2C markets, and its impact on consumer decisions. That does not necessarily mean that measuring the impact of social media on a brand's health is uncomplicated.

### *6.1.1 'Vanity metrics'*

Many aspects of social media can be measured using numbers. Yet, not all of them measure anything really important from the point of view of a brand's health. Apart from sentiment (covered in Section 6.1.3), we can measure (*The Short Guide to Measuring Not Counting* 2014):

1. Number of followers/fans or those who 'liked' our fan page. These are easy to count and have initial face validity (comments on it in a moment).

DOI: 10.4324/9781003167235-6

2. Reach is a measure of the percentage of the target audience able to see or interact with the branded content. It says nothing about the effects on the audience reached.
3. Volume (amount of posts, tweets, shares and retweets) is relatively easy to measure, yet it says nothing about the impact on brand sales, image, liking, awareness, etc.
4. Time spent on content that takes time to consume fully (such as videos, games or longer posts) might be a component of engagement and, as such, is interesting to measure.
5. Engagement is a derived measure, based on who is sharing, commenting on, retweeting, liking, linking or viewing. This metric depends on the social media platform, and in many cases is supplied by an outside third party. Most importantly, engagement can be used to measure the effectiveness of a brand's communication, but not the brand's health as such.

Many metrics used in measuring social media are called 'vanity metrics', for example: fans, followers and likes. Those metrics look impressive 'on paper', have a tendency to increase indefinitely, and are quite easy to come by, yet they are easy to manipulate and they have no relation to sales or a brand's market position. Of course, they can surely soothe the vanity of the brand owner (Bendle et al. 2016). Having many followers or fans seems great, but we do not know whether they are current or potential customers, or maybe current or potential employees, or maybe competitors trying to distort the picture of how our brand is doing. So, what exactly is a large number of followers telling us about the brand? Increasing volumes of posts or tweets seem great but try to recall the outpouring of negative reactions to flight cancellations and problems with refunds that many customers of low-cost carriers posted about on Facebook and Twitter in summer 2020 (during the Covid-19 pandemic). Can we reasonably assume that huge volumes of posts on social media are always desirable? Vanity metrics are gathered just because they are easily available, not because they tell us anything about a brand's health, nor help in making decisions regarding brand building.

Next, as Borel and Christodoulides (2016) explain, various metrics used to analyze the so-called electronic word-of-mouth (eWOM) do not facilitate their *precise attribution* to sales, nor do they facilitate the assessment of social media effectiveness. In the past, great importance was attached to the likes that brands won on Facebook. The value of likes was defined as the difference between the average shopping basket (with costs excluded, which seems to be a mistake) of brand fans (brand followers or consumers who liked the brand), and the average shopping basket of non-fans. Sometimes, it was mistakenly assumed that this difference resulted from communication activities on social media. And yet, fans of the brand are more favourable to it, and by definition more actively talk about it on social media. If previous positive experiences with a brand have an impact on its liking, it is wrong to attribute this influence to social media activities. Consumers like a brand because they are satisfied with it and not because they gave the brand a 'like' (Bendla and Bagga 2016). Even the most sophisticated statistical techniques do not help us in discriminating between simple correlation and a causal relation (*The Short Guide to Measuring Not Counting* 2014).

### *6.1.2 eWOM: volume or valence?*

Brands do not rely on social media alone. Relatively new research by Fay et al. (2019) of 500 leading brands of consumer goods, operating in 15 different product categories, paints a much more nuanced picture of social media's role: 9% of purchase decisions can be directly attributed to conversations about a brand on social media, while 10% can be attributed to offline exchanges between customers. The relationship between online vs. offline communications on impacting sales varies between 60 : 40 and 40 : 60. In the case of technological brands (such as Apple or Intel), the impact of offline conversations was greater than online, which only confirms the broader observation of the authors, that the purchase of more expensive brands is usually more strongly influenced by offline conversations than online chats. Offline conversations provide the opportunity for in-depth discussions of the 'pros and cons' with people you know and trust. As for those direct, face-to-face conversations about the brand, as many as two-thirds of researched consumers talked every day to at least one person about some brand. And it was often quite an ordinary, not very 'hot' brand, which is the usual topic of social media posts. Analysis also revealed that in the case of face-to-face conversations, the decision to buy a brand is strongly influenced by the number of conversations about it than so-called sentiment (difference between the number of positive and negative opinions).

According to Fay et al. (2019), in the case of social media, *sentiment* is most important, *volume* is half as important, brand content sharing is even less important and influencers' opinions are by far the least important. According to the analysis, the factor that had no direct impact on sales was sharing branded content (even a brand's ads), although it could have increased the number of conversations about the brand.

Yet, the dilemma 'sentiment or volume' has not been decidedly concluded. A meta-analysis of the many research studies carried out in the area of eWOM's impact on sales presents inconclusive inferences.

An analysis of 51 studies conducted by You et al. (2015) shows that the average elasticity of eWOM's volume is 0.236%, while eWOM's valence is 0.417%. In other words, eWOM's sentiment is supposed to be nearly twice as impactful as its volume. Additionally, a meta-analysis by Floyd et al. (2014) shows that sales elasticities calculated based on reviews valence are nearly double those calculated on reviews volume (0.69 vs. 0.35). Another meta-analysis carried out by Babić et al. (2016) of 96 studies indicates that the volume of eWOM has a stronger impact on sales than valence!

You et al. (2015) emphasize that the volume of eWOM has a strong impact on sales in the case of durable goods, because high prices raise the risk of making a wrong decision. Both eWOM's volume and valence are important for products that are difficult to examine before purchase, as well as for those where other consumers cannot be observed while using the products. A stronger impact of eWOM is to be expected in the case of tangible goods that have just been introduced to the market, where the role of eWOM is to reduce purchase risk. Both eWOM's volume and valence would have a much weaker impact on sales in strongly competitive categories, due to the number of offers that are difficult to compare.

Next, regarding the relationship between likes and sales, it is not known whether it is the large volume of eWOM that makes the brand sell better or the opposite: that a well-selling brand is therefore more often commented on. And analogously to the sentiment of eWOM, it might be true that brands with higher sales generate more positive opinions, and not that a positive eWOM influences higher sales of the brand. Probably if it were otherwise (the majority of opinions were critical), those brands would not sell so well. It appears that the volume of brand recommendations tends to increase with an increase in the brand's market share, which should not be surprising. The vast majority of recommendations are given to brands that consumers use, especially in the case of positive opinions. As much as 60%–80% of positive reviews given by consumers concern the most often used brand. Therefore, if a brand has more users (higher penetration), it will most likely appear among the most often recommended brands. Negative opinions are usually given to brands used in the past or brands not used at all. In their case, there is no relationship between the market share of the brand and the number of negative opinions (East et al. 2008).

Table 6.1 illustrates the problem explored here. It is impossible to explain the differences in the market share of leading smartphone brands in Poland, limiting

**TABLE 6.1** Top 5 smartphone brands in Poland, their mentions in the context of smartphones, on the Polish internet and the distribution of sentiment

| *Brands* | *Volume market share in Q4 2020 (according to Canalys) (%)* | *Mentions in the last four months of 2020* | *Percentage of neutral* | *Percentage of positive* | *Percentage of negative* |
|---|---|---|---|---|---|
| Xiaomi (incl. Redmi, Poco) | 26 | 2,043 | 48.9 | 36.7 | 14.4 |
| Apple (incl. iPhone) | 18 | 1,091 | 47.1 | 32.6 | 20.3 |
| Huawei | 14 | 2,305 | 52.3 | 33.0 | 14.7 |
| Samsung | 13 | 2,540 | 55.9 | 32.9 | 11.2 |
| Lenovo | 10 | 267 | 61.0 | 31.5 | 7.5 |

Sources: Own calculations based on Telepolis (2021) and Brand24 (access to this platform was provided by courtesy of Michal Sadowski, founder and CEO of Brand24).

the factors that might have an impact on those brands to just the volume or valence of eWOM.

Maybe the explanation lies in the nature of many (the majority?) of the comments, posts or reviews. They do not explore so much the unique nature of each brand as the desirable or unwelcome attributes of a product. When a user expresses his/her disappointment with a particular model of smartphone because it is 'clumsy', 'too wide' or 'hard to handle with just one hand', it really says nothing about a particular brand. No matter the brand, if you purchase a smartphone with a huge screen that is too wide for your hand to grasp comfortably, you might feel disappointed. When a user is satisfied because the phone has a 3.5 mm jack, this again says nothing about a particular brand. In the portfolio of every manufacturer, one may find models with that feature. Unfortunately, very few users give any suggestions regarding those attributes that cannot be checked before purchasing, such as lags, occasional slowdowns, problems with servicing or incorrect translations of the interface into local languages. Troubles with useless from the branding perspective comments, posts or reviews is not restricted to that product category. It seems that many users reviewing a particular product or service reflect on the choice they've made, showing their disappointment with those attributes (e.g. hotel located too far from the nearest metro station) that could be easily checked in advance. In other words, those reviews or comments teach readers about choice criteria but do not help in selecting the right brand.

An analysis by You et al. (2015) of 339 eWOM volume sales elasticities shows that as much as half of them are below 0.1% (or even negative!). Among 271 eWOM valence sales elasticities, over one-third are negative, which means that the better the sentiment, the lower the sales of the brand! In the analysis by Babić et al. (2016), in about two-thirds of cases, elasticities are below average. As you can see, the average values established in different studies are *not representative at all*.

eWOM 'works' especially if it comes from sources with a high level of trust that is attributed to the altruistic motivation of the reviewer. Babić et al. (2016) relate the effectiveness of eWOM with consumers' perceived similarity to the source of the brand recommendation on social media, although the perceived similarity is not necessary for e-commerce platforms.

The majority of studies concentrate on eWOM's volume vs. valence impact on sales, yet other aspects of brand mentions are worth considering. Readers of reviews or product recommendations are also influenced by the standard of grammar and spelling with which comments are written. This helps in making assumptions about the kind of people who have written them (*The Short Guide to Measuring Not Counting* 2014).

In light of the above, we have focused on sentiment analysis alone. It can be as simple as 'percentage of positive mentions minus percentage of negative mentions' (see Section 6.1.2), which is provided by many services (e.g. Socialbakers, Sprout Social, Hootsuite and Brand24). Or, it might be more elaborate, as in the case of the Brand Advocacy Index and the Brand Advocacy Ratio (described in Sections 6.2 and 6.3).

### 6.1.3 Social media sentiment

**Metric definition**

Social media sentiment is a metric that reveals how customers are talking about a brand on social media.

**Metric calculation**

$$\begin{aligned}\text{Social media sentiment}\\ &= \text{percentage of positive posts and comments regarding a brand} \\ &\quad - \text{percentage of negative posts and comments regarding a brand}\end{aligned} \tag{6.1}$$

**Metric interpretation**

Social media sentiment can take a value from –100 (if all comments and posts regarding the brand are negative) to +100 (in the opposite case). Of course, the closer the score of the sentiment of a brand is to 100, the better.

**Case**

*An analysis of posts and comments on Facebook from Polish customers of two courier companies (GLS and UPS) and Polish Post (Poczta Polska), carried out in the period between December 2019 and June 2020, revealed that among the three analyzed profiles, users' posts only appeared on the GLS one and there were many of them. For 106 posts published by GLS, another 122 were added by users. More posts appeared in the weeks leading up to Christmas and also in January/February 2020. As for their sentiment, it was rather negative. It is, however, rare for users to publish positive posts (contrary to comments) on their own. For example, in the second week of December 2019, more than three-fourths of posts were negative. As for comments, most of them were published in early December and mid-March (beginning of the pandemic) – about 100 a week, and in May/June (Mother and Father's Day competition) – up to 200 a week. During winter and at the beginning of the year, there were more negative comments, but during the competition on the occasion of Mother and Father's Day, most comments were positive. In the last week of June 2020, two-thirds of the comments were positive. Compared with UPS and Poczta Polska, many more positive and neutral comments (mainly due to competitions in May and June 2020) were posted on the GLS profile.*

*In the first half of December 2019, i.e. during the pre-holiday rush, users posted many more comments on the UPS profile than during the rest of the analyzed period. Another significant increase in the number of comments was recorded in March 2020, right after the introduction of the lockdown in Poland. The number of comments increased until mid-May. The sentiment analysis showed that the vast majority of the comments were negative. Some weeks, users published two to three times more negative comments (in the last week of*

*November 2019 all comments were negative) than neutral ones, and only single comments were positive.*

*The profile with the most comments belonged to Poczta Polska. Users posted many comments in the pre-Christmas period (over 1,000 comments were published on the website in one week in December 2019 alone). In March 2020, when the national lockdown was announced, the activity of commentators increased considerably, and the number of comments published each week exceeded that of the pre-Christmas period by several times. A significant increase was also recorded in mid-April. In February and March, as the number of comments increased, the percentage of negative and neutral ones increased significantly. Poczta Polska, like other profiles, collected very few positive comments, but the number of comments classified as negative was similar or slightly smaller than neutral ones. For example, in the last week of March 2020, almost half of the comments were neutral. The most common negative comments on the Poczta Polska profile dealt with delays in delivering letters and lack of appropriate disinfectants or gloves in the branches (Zylka 2020).*

*When analyzing sentiment for those three brands, one had to bear in mind standard proportions of positive vs. negative comments and posts. From mid-August 2020 to mid-February 2021, in the case of the 39 strongest brands in Poland (according to Superbrands Polska 2020 edition), on average only 36.8% of posts were positive versus 63.2% negative.*[1]

**Metric limitations**

As to the sentiment analysis, one of the major problems stems from using either machine learning or the lexicographic method, which seems to be more popular (Medhat et al. 2014). The problem with the second approach is that some adjectives used to describe the brand, and analyzed by the above-mentioned tools, might have both positive and negative meanings, depending on the context (e.g. funny, lofty, extravagant), so additional contextual analysis is required. What is more, a quick glance at any site with customers' opinions and comments about hotels, cars or smartphones reveals that many of them are far from being clear-cut positive or negative. From Table 6.1, we can see that 50%–60% of mentions (in the case of leading smartphone brands) are neutral. Additionally, some reviewers or commentators make spelling mistakes, use slang or make sarcastic comments, making a whole analysis even more complicated.

## 6.2 Brand Advocacy Index

**Metric definition**

*Brand Advocacy Index* is a metric of eWOM's sentiment, suggested by the Boston Consulting Group (BCG) a few years ago. It is based on two assumptions: (1) spontaneous opinions are twice as important as solicited ones ('just wanted to ask >what do you think about ...<?') and (2) critical[2] opinions are twice[3] as important as positive[4] ones (Esquivivas et al. 2013; YouTube 2018).

## Metric calculation

$$\text{Brand Advocacy Index} = \begin{pmatrix} \text{percentage of spontaneous positive recommendations} \\ +0.5 \star \text{ percentage of positive solicited recommendations} \end{pmatrix} - \begin{pmatrix} 2 \star \text{ percentage of spontaneous critical opinions} \\ + \text{percentage of critical solicited opinions} \end{pmatrix} \quad (6.2)$$

The BAI takes into account both the opinions expressed by buyers of the brand and consumers who express their opinions on various brands, although they have never purchased them (that happens, for example, in the case of cars and smartphones). The BAI can be calculated using many of the tools available to social media managers.

## Metric interpretation

The value of the BAI metric can range from –200 (all opinions about the brand are negative and spontaneous at the same time) to +100 (all opinions about the brand are positive and spontaneous at the same time). BCG research (carried out in five developed Western countries) indicates that some product categories (cars, smartphones) have a significantly higher BAI (51 and 46, respectively) than service brands, such as banks (10) and mobile operators (20). Interestingly, cars differ from banks only by twice as high a percentage of 'brand ambassadors', yet at the same time by a fourfold higher percentage of critics (Esquivivas et al. 2013; YouTube 2018).

BCG research of over 300 brands in 12 categories indicates a very strong correlation (Pearson's value of 81%) between the BAI and an increase in the revenue of the brand owner. Sales increase of brands with the highest BAI is on average 25% higher, compared to brands with the lowest BAI (Esquivivas et al. 2013; YouTube 2018).

## Metric limitations

An unequivocal distinction between a spontaneous and a solicited opinion is pretty subjective. When a consumer asks for opinions before purchasing a new smartphone, and mentions a few brands that he/she considers buying, or definitely excludes one or two, how should we categorize an opinion about a brand in various situations: when a brand is included in the consideration set ('which of the three brands X, Y or Z should I buy?') vs. not in the consideration set but also not excluded from it ('which smartphone below 400 euros would you recommend?') vs. excluded by the asking consumer ('I would definitely not buy any smartphone by brand Z'), yet strongly recommended by some of the reviewers? In which cases do we have 'spontaneous' and in which 'solicited' opinions?

Next, you need to remember that the BAI does not take into account the volume of eWOM that a brand generates. One may doubt brand X's advantage over brand Y just because its BAI is 40 vs. 35 for its competitor, if brand Y has five times as many mentions as brand X.

## 6.3 Brand Advocacy Ratio

Based on the spontaneous recommendations of customers is another metric called the *Brand Advocacy Ratio* (Kotler et al. 2017).

**Metric interpretation**

The Brand Advocacy Ratio analyzes how effectively awareness of a brand is transformed into brand recommendations.

**Metric calculation**

$$\begin{aligned}&\text{Brand Advocacy Ratio}\\&\quad=\text{number/percentage of consumers who spontaneously}\\&\qquad\text{recommend the brand : number/percentage of consumers}\\&\qquad\text{spontaneously recalling the brand}\end{aligned}\tag{6.3}$$

The BAR can be easily calculated if, in surveys, we ask how many category buyers know the brand and whether they have recommended it. Thus, if 40% of category buyers spontaneously mention the brand and 4% of them admit to spontaneously recommending it, then the BAR is 0.1. In other words, for every 10 category buyers familiar with the brand, only 1 has recommended it spontaneously.

**Metric interpretation**

The values of the BAR metric range from 0 to 1 and the closer to 1, the more ready to recommend the brand are customers who are aware of it. We might expect the BAR to be closer to 1 in the case of specialized, niche brands. If the BAR is close to 0, it is worth exploring the problem by asking 'why, even though they know us, they do not recommend our brand?' There can be several answers to that question.

**Metric limitations**

A low BAR score cannot be unmistakably interpreted. Consumers might have their own favourite brand, other than the one explored. It may be that the brand is OK, but it does not impress customers. Maybe the product is very good, but customer service is just so-so. Maybe the reason behind a low BAI is the low involvement product category, in which it is difficult to count on spontaneous recommendations. Or maybe the consumer does not feel an expert in a given category to recommend brands. Each of these responses requires the brand owner to take different actions.

## Recommendations for brand managers

1. B2C brands, no matter how active on social media, should analyze the Brand Advocacy Index, bearing in mind that it does not take into account the volume of eWOM. Discussions are ongoing whether eWOM's volume is more important than its valence (sentiment), or just the opposite.
2. When conducting surveys aimed at measuring brand awareness, it makes sense to add the question regarding brand recommendations. It will allow you to calculate the Brand Advocacy Ratio. If it is close to 0, you should further explore the reasons for it.

## Questions

1. Why are negative opinions given the double weight of positive ones (in the Brand Advocacy Index)?
2. Why are spontaneous opinions in the Brand Advocacy Index given the double weight of solicited ones?
3. When can the percentage of consumers being aware of the brand that recommend it, be low ?

# Notes

1 Own estimations based on Brand24. Access to this platform was provided by courtesy of Michal Sadowski, founder and CEO of Brand24.

2 The tendency to give negative recommendations is stronger in services, which arises from the difficulty of providing consumers with repeat, positive and distinctive experiences with the service brand.

3 This is because customers who criticize the brand usually share their opinion with an audience twice as large as those who praise it.

4 It has been proved that the tendency to give positive recommendations to a brand is higher in product categories (a) with a strong emotional element; (b) of aspirational value, where consumption is socially visible; and (c) with a high price, where product purchase requires a lot of time. According to BCG research in eight countries around the world, on a sample of over 200,000 respondents, motives for giving positive recommendations to the brand are (Esquivivas et al. 2013; YouTube 2018): (1) in services (car insurance, mobile telecoms, internet providers, retail chains) mainly three factors with more or less equal impact: satisfaction with the service, good value for money and customer service; (2) in the case of cars (with the exception of prestigious brands) and smartphones, satisfaction with the product is key, followed by good value for money (more important for cars) and a strong emotional bond with the brand (number two in smartphones and number three in cars), and the least important is customer service; and (3) in retail banking, customer service is key, and the other factors (offer, value for money and emotional bond) are more or less equally important.

# Literature

Babić Rosaria A., Sotgiu F., de Valck K., Bijmolt T.H.A., 2016, The Effect of Electronic Word of Mouth on Sales: A Meta-Analytic Review of Platform, Product, and Metric Factors, *Journal of Marketing Research*, Vol. LIII, pp. 297–318, doi: 10.1509/jmr.14.0380.

Bendle N.T., Bagga Ch.K., 2016, The Metrics That Marketers Muddle, *MIT Sloan Management Review*, Spring, S. 73–81.

Borel L.-H., Christodoulides G., 2016, Branding and Digital Analytics, in: *The Routledge Companion to Contemporary Brand Management*, ed. F. Dall'Olmo Riley, J. Singh, Ch. Blankson, Routledge, London, pp. 255–268.

East R., Wright M., Vanhuele M., 2008, *Consumer Behaviour: Applications in Marketing*, SAGE, Los Angeles.

Esquivivas P., Knox S., Sanchez-Rodriguez V., Visser J., 2013, Fueling Growth Through Word of Mouth: Introducing the Brand Advocacy Index, *The Boston Consulting Group*, December.

Fay B., Keller E., Larkin R., Pauwels K., 2019, Deriving Value From Conversations About Your Brand, *MIT Sloan Management Review*, Winter, pp. 72–77.

Floyd K., Freling R., Alhoqail S., Young Cho H., Freling T., 2014, How Online Product Reviews Affect Retail Sales: A Meta-analysis, *Journal of Retailing*, 90(2), pp. 217–232, doi: 10.1016/j.jretai.2014.04.004.

Kotler Ph, Kartajaya H., Setiawan I., 2017, *Marketing 4.0: Moving from Traditional to Digital*, John Wiley & Sons, Hoboken, NJ.

Medhat W., Hassan A., Korashy H., 2014, Sentiment Analysis Algorithms and Applications: A Survey, *Ain Shams Engineering Journal*, 5, pp. 1093–1113, doi: 10.1016/j.asej.2014.04.011.

Telepolis, 2021, www.telepolis.pl/wiadomosci/prawo-finanse-statystyki/canalys-rynek-smartfonow-w-polsce-4q2020-xiaomi-apple-huawei-samsung.

*The Short Guide to Measuring Not Counting: How to Evaluate Social Media for Marketing Communications*, 2014, IPA Social Works, London.

You Y., Vadakkepatt J.A.M., 2015, A Meta-Analysis of Electronic Word-of-Mouth Elasticity, *Journal of Marketing*, 79, pp. 19–39, doi: 10.1509/jm.14.0169.

YouTube, 2018, *The Brand Advocacy Index (BAI)*, www.youtube.com/watch?v=b6ZJGlHyv7s, published on: 11 September [access: 6.12.2019].

Zylka K., 2020, Czy komentarze na Facebooku szkodza wizerunkowi Twojej marki? Case Study Firm kurierskich, *Sotrender*, 3 November, www.sotrender.com/blog/pl/2020/11/sentyment-komentarzy-case-study-firm-kurierskich/ [access: 18.01.2021].

# 7

# HOLISTIC METRICS OF A BRAND'S HEALTH

**Learning objectives:**

After reading this chapter you should:

- understand the drawbacks of sales analysis and the need for market share analysis;
- be familiar with four holistic metrics of a brand's market strength: market share, Purchase Activation Ratio (PAR), brand contribution and a brand's surplus margin (BSM), of which the last two are of a financial nature;
- be able to critically analyze metrics that constitute a brand's market share from the perspective of buyers, distributors and retailers;
- be able to calculate all of the above metrics.

## 7.1 Why not just sales?

The metrics covered in Chapters 1–6 are useful for analyzing branding outcomes along successive stages of a customer's journey. In order to have the 'big picture' of a brand's health, we need other measures. Paradoxically, a brand's sales should *not* be the most important measure. But why? After all, when a brand's sales are increasing, there should be no doubt about its market success. Yet, this assumption is wrong.

A brand can grow, even in the long term (sales increase in the following way: 10 → 11 → 13 → 15), but the market in which it competes could have grown much faster at the same time (total market: 100 → 120 → 150 → 200). Therefore, despite the significant increase in the brand's sales (50%) in just three years, the brand may be weaker in the fourth year than it was at the beginning.

What's more, in planning the marketing activities for a brand, the information that its current sales are 50 or 500 is not sufficient because the strategy of

DOI: 10.4324/9781003167235-7

a brand achieving a sales level of 50 in a market of 100 will be different than a brand selling 500, but competing in a market worth 5,000. It is not so much the nominal value of sales but rather sales relative to other players that should guide strategic recommendations for a brand's growth.

Case studies in the Institute of Practitioners in Advertising (IPA) databank (prepared for the IPA Effectiveness Awards) show that campaigns focusing on sales tend to underperform, having the lowest overall success rate in terms of effectiveness (across every business metric) and accountability. Campaigns focused on market share gain are more effective, on every business metric (Binet and Field 2007).

Another advantage of analyzing market share is its lower (as opposed to sales) sensitivity to seasonal fluctuations in demand. Since beer and ice cream brands usually increase their sales significantly during summer and decrease in periods of colder weather, analyzing a brand's sales data throughout the year may lead to the erroneous conclusion that its market position is constantly changing. However, since the weather affects the demand for all beer and ice cream brands, analyzing their market share eliminates the impact of this factor, as well as all other factors affecting the seasonal fluctuations of sales (East et al. 2008). According to a meta-analysis of over 400 studies, market share generally tends to be stable over time,[1] so generating sustained long-term growth of market share in mature markets is usually difficult (Dekimpe and Hanssens 1995).

## 7.2 Brand's market share and its components

**Definition**: *A brand's* ***share of the market*** *is used for a reliable assessment of the competitive position of the brand, eliminating the impact of factors influencing the seasonal fluctuations of sales.*

**Metric calculation**

Brand's market share = 100 * brand sales (volume/value) : total category sales (volume/value) (7.1)

If we use the number of units sold, we obtain the volume market share, and if we use dollar sales, we arrive at the value market share. If we divide the value market share for the brand by the volume market share (and multiply the quotient by 100), we obtain the so-called 'brand price index'.[2]

**Case**

*The volume and value market shares of three beer brands in Poland are presented in Table 7.1. We can easily calculate the price indices for those brands. Between 2018 and 2019, all those indices decreased: in the case of Lech Premium from 110 to 107.5; in the case of Tyskie Gronie from 104 to 103; and in the case of Zubr from 91 to 90.*

The calculation of market share entails several problems.

First of all, it is necessary to precisely define the market, both in terms of products and geography. A too narrow definition of the market in product

**TABLE 7.1** Volume and value market shares of three beer brands in 2018 and 2019

| *Brand* | *Cumulated period January–December 2018* | | *Cumulated period January–December 2019* | |
|---|---|---|---|---|
| | *Volume % share* | *Value % share* | *Volume % share* | *Value % share* |
| Lech Premium | 4.1 | 4.5 | 4.0 | 4.3 |
| Tyskie Gronie | 10.2 | 10.6 | 10.2 | 10.5 |
| Żubr | 13.9 | 12.6 | 13.4 | 12.1 |

Source: Kompania Piwowarska SA sourced from NielsenIQ, Retail Audit, Total Poland incl. Discounters (Beer), category: beer.

terms (chocolate bars with a peanut filling of 50 g) reduces the number of competitors included in the denominator of the formula, thereby artificially overestimating the market share of the examined brand. On the other hand, a too wide (sweets in general) market delineation will unnecessarily expand the number of products taken into account, and thus the number of competitors, which results in a significantly underestimated market share. The solution may be to use industry-wide categorizations, but the best option would be to look at the product category boundaries through the eyes of the consumer (see Section 1.1.1). When he/she wants to satisfy a specific need, what products does he/she usually consider?

The same problem applies to the geographical reach of a brand. It makes no sense to calculate a brand's share in the nationwide market if it is only available in one region of the country. But it is also inappropriate to accept as 'the market' only those stores or distributors where the brand is available and to estimate its market share based on the sales of those intermediaries. As we know, the metrics thus calculated are referred to as share-in-shops-handling (see Section 3.1.2).

Let us add here, that if a brand is present in several different categories, or offered in different markets, its shares should be determined for each separately, and therefore the above dilemmas have to be resolved several times.

Next, it is important to use the actual sales at store level in the nominator. The point is not to determine market share based on sales to intermediaries, because there is no guarantee that goods will not return to the supplier. When it comes to determining the volume of sales to end users, you cannot rely on respondents' declarations in market surveys because even if they can correctly indicate the brand bought within the category, they will definitely not specify the number of packages or the value of purchases per year. What is more, consumer surveys (declared purchases) tend to be biased towards well-known brands (Bendle et al. 2016). The only solution is to reach for market statistics offered by market research companies. For fast-moving consumer goods (FMCG) industries, those can be store audits (Nielsen); in many categories of durable goods there are trade associations providing such information, while in services the problem does not occur. In the case of services, there are no intermediaries or the possibility of storing goods in warehouses and therefore there is no risk of obtaining an unrealistic picture of the market position of the brand, due to the inclusion in the nominator of the service 'waiting on the shelves' for the buyer.

Finally, in the case of the volume market share there is a problem of package comparability (size of jars of jams, yogurt cups, etc.). In order to calculate the volume market share, in the case of FMCG it will be necessary to include not quantities of packages sold but their tonnage or volume. On the other hand, in the case of the value market share, in many categories in which sellers commonly offer rebates or discounts (e.g. sales of cars or apartments), there is a problem in determining 'at what price' the value of sales was calculated. Transaction prices are, of course, possible to determine. It is also important to include transaction prices in the denominator of Formula 7.1 (sales for the entire industry).

**Cases**

(1) *In 2017, Nike's share value in the US sneakers market was 32.9%, while no. 2 Adidas had just 10.3% (Ringen 2018).*

(2) *In May 2020, the Polish market for fabric softeners was dominated by three brands: Lenor (36% share value); Coccolino (20%); and Silan (19%) (Coccolino 2020).*

(3) *In 2020, Amazon had a 38.7% share value in US e-commerce. No 2 was Walmart (5.3%) and no. 3 was eBay (4.7%) (Meyer 2020).*

(4) *In 1995, Tesco became leader of the UK retail market, overcoming Sainsbury's, which had market shares of around 18%. From that moment on, Tesco's share steadily increased, while Sainsbury's decreased, so that in 2003, ASDA had become no. 2 in the UK. In 2009, Tesco was a distant leader of the market with a ca. 32% share, no. 2 was ASDA and no. 3 Sainsbury's; both with shares of around 17%, and no. 4 was Morrisons with a ca. 13% share (Gregory and Parnum 2020).*

## Alternative formulas for market share calculation

Parfitt and Collins (1968) presented a very helpful formula for calculating the volume market share (in the case of value, the product in Formula 7.2 should be multiplied by the price index). It is based on metrics known to us from previous chapters, namely:

Market share = penetration rate ⋆ share of wallet ⋆ heavy usage index[3] (±1) (7.2)

Formula 7.2 may also apply to durable goods. The only difference in this case is a longer period than a year that must be analyzed.[4]

A brand's market share may be calculated not only from the perspective of its final customers but also from the perspective of distributors that offer the brand. In this case, the market share is the product of[5]

Brand market share = weighted distribution ⋆ share-in-shops-handling (7.3)

Both metrics may be expressed in volume or value terms.

### Case

*Guinness is a famous Irish dark stout beer, with over 160 years of history. In 2018, in its home market, 82% of Guinness sales came from pubs with the remaining 18% from so-called 'in-home' consumption. In 2016, the weighted distribution of Guinness Draught in Irish pubs was an astounding 99.6%, which means that practically every pub in Ireland (at that time there were nearly 7,200) offered that brand. Guinness share-in-pubs-handling was a healthy 32.5%, even though an average pub in Ireland offered 50 brands (in 2018 – a huge increase from just 36 the year before). The brand's value market share in Ireland for the years 2012–2019 was nearly constant (around 25%). In the UK, in turn, 71% of Guinness sales (in 2018) came from pubs vs. 29% from 'in-home' drinking. Guinness had (in 2017) a 66.3% weighted distribution in pubs in the UK (in 2018 it dropped to 64.2%), and a 5.3% value market share (Gallery and Sor 2016; Stoney 2018; Stoney and Mawdsley 2020).*

In the case of retail chains, the formula for their value market share looks different[6]:

Retailer's value market share = penetration rate * relative frequency of visits * relative receipt (7.4)

where the relative frequency of visits is the average number of visits per customer[7] (in a specified time period) in retailer X's stores divided by the average number of visits per customer in stores of a particular trade; relative receipt is the average receipt in retailer X's stores divided by the average receipt in stores of a particular trade.

### Case

*In a highly competitive UK retail market, it took German discount chain Lidl 10 years to achieve a 3.5% share (in 2014). Three years later, its share rose to 5.1% and Lidl was going head-to-head with Waitrose. In those three years, household penetration rose from 47.8% to 53.9%. In 2017, Lidl's UK sales index was 273, while in 2008 it was 100, to which the following factors contributed: an increase in the penetration index (from 100 to 355); an increase in the basket size (receipt) index (by 32%); and an increase in the frequency index (by 23%) (Clouder 2018). As we can see, penetration's growth contribution into sales growth was considerably greater than the increase in the basket size or the frequency of visits.*

### Metric interpretation

A brand's market share calculated for a specified period of time (year, half-year) illustrates the competitive position of the brand in that period. Definitely, it is better to analyze market share in dynamic terms because it allows you to answer the question whether a brand is strengthening its position in the market, or is it weakening against the background of the entire industry or a key competitor.

### Case

*In little more than 10 years from Chobani's debut (in 2007) on the US yogurt market, the brand outstripped its major rivals (Yoplait, Danone) and claimed a 19% share of the market, and 43% of the Greek yogurt market (Paynter 2019).*

Davis (2018) rightly suggests to analyze factors that have influenced market share decline, and in situations of share increase, to check whether that change is sustainable. He also warns against market share increases which are a by-product of an ageing category, in which case smarter suppliers have exited, leaving more space for the remaining competitors whose market shares grow automatically.

**Case**

*John Lewis, a famous British department store, known for nostalgic, heart-warming Christmas ads increased its market share from ca. 22.5% in fiscal year 2010 to 29.6% in 2016 and 32% in 2019. John Lewis is the only major department stores that, in the years 2010–2019, has witnessed constant year-on-year revenue growth during Christmas, which accounts for ca. 20% of annual sales and 40% of annual profits (Wood 2020). Undoubtedly, the impressive (10 percentage points) growth of a brand's share in a mature market, within just 10 years is rare. At the same time, it signalled problems that department stores were encountering in those years. In 2012, a major competitor was forced to close. The rise of e-tailers has also forced many other department stores to close (Debenhams and BHS), while others have been compelled to close some outlets (John Lewis among them) (Butler 2020). The same problems face department stores in the United States. In 2020, three major department stores (Neiman Marcus, JCPenney and Lord & Taylor) filed for bankruptcy (Stone 2020). Troubles for department stores were already obvious in the early 1990s: in 1993, their share of overall US retail sales was 14.4%, which declined to 12.6% in 1999, 7.5% in 2008 and 3.7% in 2019 (a year before the coronavirus pandemic) (Lahart 2020).*

In the case of strongly competitive product categories, in which all rivals offer relatively homogeneous products, it can be assumed with a high degree of probability that brands with small market shares do not generate a profit for their owners or, at most, their profits are minuscule. Szymanski's et al. (1993) analysis, covering 49 studies (reporting 276 econometric models), shows that there is a *positive correlation between market share and company profits*. Many other analyses indicate that market share is correlated with profitability, yet it is not a cause and effect relationship. Of course, in those markets where economies of scale operate, building a larger market share is undoubtedly beneficial because it reduces the unit costs and therefore translates into higher profitability (Bendle and Bagga 2016).

As to the question of 'what high market share means', everything depends on the number of competitors in the industry. The situation is different in highly fragmented industries, in which hundreds of brands are available. Here, a market share of 5% can be a huge success. We find a completely different situation in an industry with a few competing brands (this is often the case in B2B industries), where the smallest of them may have 10% of the market.

**Cases**

(1) *British car and home direct insurance markets are good examples of very crowded categories. Leading brands have relatively low and very similar market shares (data for*

*2012). In the case of car insurance, leaders in the market share at the time were Aviva/NU – 8.3%; Direct Line – 7.7%; Admiral – 6.9%; Liverpool Victoria – 6.8%; and Tesco – 5.2%. In the case of home direct insurance, the top 5 brands were: Aviva – 7.0%; Halifax – 6.1%; Direct Line – 5.5%; Lloyds – 4.7%; and Churchill – 4.7% (Bratton et al. 2016).*

(2) *Another example of a highly fragmented market, with the majority of brands with low market shares, is cars. In 2015, out of the top 30 brands of cars in the UK, 23 had volume market shares below 5%. For example, Suzuki's share at that time was just 1.3%. After two years of intensive advertising, Suzuki's share had risen to 1.6%. By the way, at that time, Suzuki's consideration score was at a record high level for that brand, at 44% (Courtney et al. 2018).*

In light of the above deliberations, market share should be assessed *relatively*, in relation to the largest, or perceived as a key competitor. Such relative market share, as it is easy to see, can be calculated without sales data for the entire industry. It is enough to divide the sales (value or volume) of a given brand by the sales of its key competitor. A relative market share above 1 is obviously a reason for satisfaction, while a value closer to 0 proves the weak competitive standing of our brand.

**Case**

*In the British premium cars segment of the market, in 2000 Audi had a relative market share of 0.5 (compared with BMW). In 2014, it became the leader of the segment, with a market share of 6.4%. Yet at that time, Audi sold cars at prices considerably lower than BMW and Mercedes (–14% in the case of the latter). In 2017, Audi managed to maintain its leading position in the premium cars segment, with 6.9% market share, and a narrowing price gap (only 5% below the price of Mercedes cars) (Lion 2018).*

Knowledge of a brand's market share allows you to objectively assess its position against competitors; however, without further analysis, it does not allow you to answer the question about the origin of this status nor to discover how to strengthen that standing. The information that the volume market share is 10% and that it has increased by 0.2 percentage point from last year, and that the relative share (relative to the largest rival) is 1.25 does not explain *why* it is so, nor does it indicate what to do next. *It is not so that two brands with the same market shares should have exactly the same market strategy*, as we will see in a moment.

### 7.2.1 Detailed analysis of market share components

Decomposing share into prime factors (as in Formula 7.2) allows you to diagnose more accurately the reasons for the increase (or decline) in a brand's market share. It might be caused by one (or a few) of the following reasons:

1. an increasing (decreasing) percentage of category buyers who buy a particular brand;

2. a shift in the demand reported by current brand buyers – increasing (decreasing) share of wallet;
3. a disproportionate increase (decrease) in product purchases, made by current brand buyers.

Analyses of the successes and failures of new brands prove that a year after entering the market those brands that achieved low sales, as a rule, recorded *increases* in penetration rates, average purchase frequency and repetition of purchases *between the first and second quarter*. In the second quarter, those metrics had reached their maximum values, after which they began to decline from the third quarter on. Brands that have been successful from the very beginning, *recorded an increase in penetration, purchase frequency and repetition of purchases for all subsequent quarters*, which resulted in a systematic increase in their market share (Singh and Wright 2016). An important conclusion we should draw is that it is not possible to definitely assess the success of a new brand after just four or five months of its presence on the market.

Next, you should recall that the penetration of individual brands usually varies significantly (see Section 3.2.2): market leaders can have penetration rates up to several dozen times higher than brands with small market shares. On the other hand, the differences in their share of wallet are decidedly smaller (see Section 5.5): market leaders have very similar values of share of wallet and do not differ much (maybe three or four times, at the maximum) from brands with much smaller market shares.

Let us return to Formula 7.4 for market share in the case of retailers. The relative frequency of visits mainly depends on stores' format: in discount stores or bakeries it will be higher than 1 (average number of visits per customer in a month is higher than in the case of an average store carrying foodstuffs); in hypermarket or cash-and-carry chains it will be below 1 (average number of visits per customer in a month is lower than in the case of an average store carrying FMCG). The average number of visits to discounters might be even double the number of visits to hypermarkets. Retailers may, of course, compete with other stores of a particular format on frequency of visits, but most probably the average customer of any retailer of a particular format makes much the same number of visits there (in a given period of time). In fact, market statistics prove that the average number of, for example, gasoline purchases in a four-week period, by customers of different gasoline stations is nearly identical (Jones and Slater 2003).

Next, relative receipt also depends mainly on stores' format: in convenience chains it will be much lower than 1 (average receipt is considerably lower than in the case of an average store carrying FMCG); in hypermarket or cash-and-carry chains it will be above 1 (average FMCG basket at a hypermarket is much more valuable than in the case of an average store carrying FMCG). In other words, differences in the value of an average receipt between retailers of different formats are significantly higher than differences between retailers within a given format. Of course, retailers may compete with other stores of a particular format on basket size, which depends on the assortment offered, prices, customer service and shopping experience offered, etc. Yet, differences between any two hypermarket chains will be incomparably smaller than between the most successful convenience chain and the least successful hypermarket or cash-and-carry chain.

Of course, we understand the mechanism that lies behind these tendencies – everything depends on the shopping mission. In the case of convenience stores, the majority of customers visit them quite frequently, but usually to make some complementary purchases. Therefore, relative frequency is above 1, but relative receipt is well below 1. In the case of hypermarkets, shopping trips there are to restock the pantry, so the average receipt is much higher than in smaller shops, yet the frequency of visits is much lower (relative frequency below 1). Now, if we multiply both metrics for a particular retailer, we shall see that, to some degree, those opposing tendencies will cancel one another out. When we multiply the relative frequency of above 1, by the relative receipt of below 1 (for convenience chain), and compare those with a relative frequency of below 1 multiplied by a relative receipt of above 1 (for a hypermarket chain), we get the products that do not differ that much! At least not so much, as *penetration rates for various retailers might differ*. For example, in Poland most popular retailers have a yearly penetration rate of ca. 90%, while some smaller retail chains' yearly penetration rates are just 10% or even less (out of confidentiality, the author cannot give detailed numbers here). Of course, the penetration rates mainly depend on the number of stores, and also their localities (ease of access; population size), assortment, prices, atmosferics (Kotler 1974), etc. This means that the penetration rates between the most popular and the least popular retailers might differ even 10-fold, while the product of relative frequency and relative receipt might differ two- or three-fold maximum.

We should also note that brands with small market shares are usually 'penalized' twice – by having *lower penetration and a lower share of wallet* (the so-called double jeopardy law[8]). This is because buyers of small brands usually also have larger brands (market leaders) in their repertoire, yet this does not work the other way around: buyers of market leaders do not feel the need to buy smaller brands. It looks as though the purchase of a small, not-so-well-known brand does not fully satisfy the needs and wants of customers, so they also like to buy large, well-known brands. Thus, the distribution of the purchases made by small brand customers (duplication of purchases including market leaders) naturally results in lower shares of wallet for smaller brands (Sharp 2017). It is worth noting here that the opposite situation to the 'double jeopardy law' occurs for the largest brands in a category: their higher penetration is usually accompanied by a higher (than in the case of competitors) share of wallet (Jones and Slater 2003).

Finally, it should be noted that this phenomenon is slightly different in the case of *private labels* (Ehrenberg et al. 1990). They usually have a high share in the sales of a particular retail chain (share-in-shops-handling), with a relatively low level of weighted distribution (in the best case 20% but usually just a few percent). For private labels, low penetration (resulting from limited distribution) and a relatively high share of wallet are natural. Customers shopping at a particular retailer often have a limited range of brands (especially when they shop at discount stores), and the retailer's own brands are exceptionally well exhibited. The greater the share of private labels in the offer of a given retail chain, usually the more customers are attached to it (Corstjens and Lal 2000).

## Example

Let us return to Formula 7.2. Because the average product purchases by customers of competing brands are usually similar, their heavy usage indices are close to 1, as already explained (see note 3). It can therefore be omitted, and thus we get the formula for market share reduced to the product of 'penetration' and 'share of wallet'. And what reveals the analysis of these two metrics?

Well, *two brands* competing in the same market with *identical market shares* can achieve it thanks to *varied success in acquiring and retaining customers.*

In a hypothetical example (as presented in Table 7.2), brand X attracts consumers more effectively (thanks to better availability? more effective communication? more attractive packaging? lower prices? better merchandizing?), while brand Y probably has customers who are more satisfied with the product.

The metrics from Table 7.2 can be graphically presented as in Diagram 7.1. The checkered areas illustrate market shares that are equal in both cases, although they are each time the product of different values of multipliers.

Obviously, the future strategies of these two brands should be different: the owner of brand X should work on the product and the perception of value vs.

**TABLE 7.2** Hypothetical penetration and share of wallet of two brands with identical market shares

| | *Volume market share (%)* | *Penetration (%)* | *Share of wallet (%)* |
|---|---|---|---|
| Brand X | **16** | 80 | 20 |
| Brand Y | **16** | 40 | 40 |

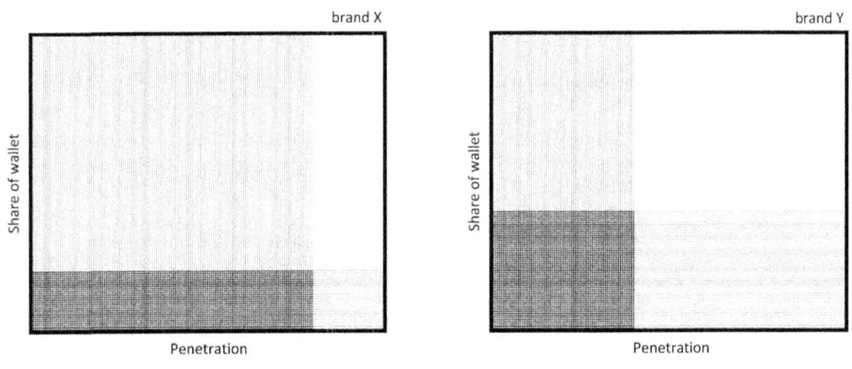


**DIAGRAM 7.1** Market share of brands X and Y as a product of penetration and share of wallet.

price, whereas the owner of brand Y should focus on improving availability, communication, packaging and merchandizing.

Let us now look at those two competitors with the same market share, but from the perspective of the brand's position in the distribution channels (see Table 7.3). What is the diagnosis of their current market situation? What suggestions for future actions can we provide?

As we can see, brand X is available in the majority of key (for the sales of a given product category) stores, but it generates only a quarter of the sales of the category. Brand Y is in the opposite circumstances – without doubt it dominates in the sales of the stores that offer the brand, yet its availability leaves much to be desired. Brand Y can be found on the shelves of stores responsible for only one-fifth of the total sales of the product. Therefore, the owner of brand Y should first improve its availability[9] (trade marketing), while the owner of brand X should strive to increase its sales in stores where it is already offered (by better merchandizing, more attractive packaging, perhaps lowering prices or offering promotional incentives to consumers).

To sum up, information that two brands competing in the same market achieve similar sales volumes and therefore have an identical market share says *nothing* about the effectiveness of marketing activities undertaken so far, nor about the brand's standing among customers and distributors. It also gives no suggestion of what action is desired in the future.

A complete analysis of market share and its components is needed, preferably in dynamic terms. Returning to our example, let's assume that the situation of the examined brands changed within two years, as shown in Table 7.4.

**TABLE 7.3** Hypothetical weighted distribution and share-in-shops-handling of two brands with identical market shares

| | *Volume market share (%)* | *Weighted distribution (%)* | *Share-in-shops-handling (%)* |
|---|---|---|---|
| Brand X | **16** | 64 | 25 |
| Brand Y | **16** | 20 | 80 |

**TABLE 7.4** Hypothetical metrics of two competing brands with identical market shares

| *Brand* | *Market share* | | *Penetration* | | *Share of wallet* | | *Weighted distribution* | | *Share-in-shops-handling* | |
|---|---|---|---|---|---|---|---|---|---|---|
| | *2 years ago (%)* | *Today (%)* | *2 years ago (%)* | *Today (%)* | *2 years ago (%)* | *Today (%)* | *2 years ago (%)* | *Today (%)* | *2 years ago (%)* | *Today (%)* |
| X | 17 | **16** | 81 | 80 | 21 | 20 | 60 | 64 | 28.3 | 25 |
| Y | 15 | **16** | 40 | 40 | 37.5 | 40 | 19 | 20 | 79 | 80 |

By decomposing the market share and analyzing changes in metrics over time, we start to understand what mechanisms have influenced the market standing of both brands and what needs to be improved. Brand X today has a significant advantage over brand Y in penetration; it is purchased by twice as many customers. It is worth noting that brand Y is ineffective in expanding its customer base, which appears to be due to its poor availability. Although brand X is more popular than brand Y, among customers and retailers, its position (and advantage over Y) is diluting. What's more, for some time (at least two years), brand X is not the 'brand of first choice' for its customers. Admittedly, brand X is available in the majority of important stores, but it generates only a quarter of category sales and this share has slightly decreased. For its buyers, brand X represents only 20% of purchases within the category and this metric evidently has not improved. One can guess that brand X has seen better days, staying in the shopping baskets and on store shelves more out of habit than because it offers a really unique experience. Brand Y is just the opposite – an example of a product that satisfies customers, hence the high (and growing) share-in-shops-handling, as well as the relatively high (and growing) share of wallet. Unfortunately, the owner of brand Y, apart from the product itself, does poor marketing. It has clearly not been able to convince new consumers to buy it, nor new distributors to offer it in order to improve the brand's availability. All this cannot be seen while analyzing annual sales only. Remember, both brands generate the same level of sales!

Table 7.5 summarizes major recommendations for the brand owner in the case of different configurations of major components of market share.

**Metric limitations**

Although high market share (including relative market share) is highly desirable, you should *beware* of actions aimed at increasing it *at all costs*. Armstrong and Green (2007) warn against such a strategy, stating that competitive strategies focusing on stealing market shares from rivals usually harm a brand's performance. Rather, brand owners should pursue profit than try to defeat competitors no matter what. In particular, taking away market share from rivals by lowering own prices, which sometimes leads to price wars, is considered harmful. A high correlation between market share and profit (Szymanski et al. analysis quoted earlier) does not mean that in all conditions an increase in market share will lead to an increase in profits.

What is more, some studies (Rego et al. 2013) show that, surprisingly, in B2C markets, under most circumstances, the link between market share and customer satisfaction is *negative*. In other words, activities designed to grow market share might adversely affect customer satisfaction.

### 7.2.2 Brand's vs. company's market share

A brand's market share determines the market position of its owner. In the situation of a corporate brand (the only brand that a company uses to mark its

**TABLE 7.5** Recommendations for typical combinations of metrics constituting market share

| *Penetration* | *Share of wallet* | *Weighted distribution* | *Share-in-shops-handling* | *Recommendations* |
|---|---|---|---|---|
| High | High | High | High | It looks like everything's perfect. But don't take it for granted – beware of disruptors that might completely change the rules of the game. So, monitor changes in buyers' expectations and technological, social and demographic trends. |
| High | Low | High | Low | A brand is purchased by many customers and is available in most important points of sale. Yet, it is 'one of many' in a product category, most probably satisfying the need for variety, being seldom purchased (on some specific occasions only?) or in small quantities. The brand owner should try to understand the reasons behind the low share of wallet and share-in-shops-handling, and try to reformulate the product or add some expected features/benefits. |
| High | Low | Low | High | The brand is very popular but most probably many brand buyers have problems with its poor availability. The brand sells very well in those shops that carry it, although those are not the most important points of sale for the category. Therefore, brand buyers have to substitute it with a competitor's, at least from time to time. A major task is to improve the brand's availability. |
| Low | High | High | Low | The brand has a small number of highly loyal users who have no problem with buying the brand, as it is available in many major shops. Yet, because the number of brand buyers is small, in shops where the brand is available it does not sell very well. Maybe the price is too high for the majority of potential customers? The brand owner has to increase penetration by communicating the brand's benefits to other, attractive segments of the market. Maybe there are also problems with the brand's visibility on the shelves of the stores that carry it. |
| Low | High | Low | High | The brand has a small number of highly loyal users, who know where to look for it as the brand is not available in the majority of major shops. In those few shops where the brand is available, it sells very well. The major task is to improve the brand's availability. If that is not enough to increase brand penetration, the brand owner should increase its communication efforts. |
| Low | Low | Low | Low | Either your brand is just starting over or its marketing strategy is completely ineffective. |

offering), the market share of the brand (in a category) is the same as the market share of the company.

Yet, when a company offers several brands in a given product category, targeted at different segments or offered in different distribution channels, its market share in a category is the sum of the market shares of its brands. Therefore, it would be correct to talk about 'market share of brands belonging to company X' and not 'market share of company X'. This is because buyers do not purchase the product under the name P&G, General Motors, Luxottica or Kering, but (for example) Pantene, Chevrolet, Oakley or Boucheron. It is those brands, and not the name of the owner (which is probably unknown to many customers), through the associations that consumers have built in their minds and emotions evoked by the memory of past experiences that affect the decision-making process. Therefore, instead of talking about 'P&G's share in the shampoo market', we should be talking about 'the share of P&G brands (Pantene, Aussie, Head & Shoulders, Herbal Essences) in the shampoo market'. It is thanks to these four brands, offered under their specific names, that P&G gains its market share. And only this, and no other brand configuration within this product category, generates a specific market share. Without risking the loss of a significant part of the market, P&G cannot swap brands (suddenly Pantene shampoo gets the name Aussie and vice versa) or combine them (let's say, Herbal Essences and Head & Shoulders merged to create one brand, fusing the attributes of both), or replace them all with one brand, identical to the company name. In fact, it is not P&G that 'has' those market shares, but four independent, distinctive and different brands, belonging to that company.

**Case**

*In 2018, brands of coffee belonging to Nestlé (over 20 brands, among them Nescafe and Starbucks Coffee-At-Home) had 25% of the global retail coffee sales, while brands belonging to Jacobs Douwe Egberts (over 60 brands, among them Carte Noire, Gevalia, Jacobs, Marcilla, and Maxwell House) had 12%. The third largest seller, Italian Lavazza, had some 3% of global sales (Storm in a coffee cup 2019). Clearly, the coffee market is very fragmented, with literally hundreds of local and regional brands competing on particular markets. On the other hand, the smartphone market is a truly global one. In the second quarter of 2020, just four suppliers (Huawei, Samsung, Apple, Xiaomi) had nearly two-thirds (in volume) of the global market (20.2%, 19.5%, 13.6% and 10.3%, respectively; IDC 2020). Those four companies offer just seven brands: Huawei and Honor (at the time of writing the book) in the case of Huawei; Galaxy in the case of Samsung; Redmi, POCO and Mi in the case of Xiaomi; and iPhone in the case of Apple.*

## 7.3 Purchase Activation Ratio

### Metric definition

*Purchase Activation Ratio* is the metric proposed by Kotler et al. (2017). It can be used to assess the effectiveness of marketing activities targeted at customers who already know the brand, in which case an important question arises: 'if they know the brand, are they buying it?'. The Purchase Activation Ratio PAR measures how effectively the brand owner has managed to transform consumers aware of the brand into its buyers.

### Metric calculation

Purchase Activation Ratio = number of brand buyers : number of consumers aware of a brand (7.5)

Formula 7.5 can be easily transformed, by dividing the numerator and denominator by all buyers of a given product category, resulting in two metrics we know very well:

Purchase Activation Ratio = penetration rate : spontaneous brand awareness (7.6)

The metric can be easily calculated, when the brand owner measures the penetration and brand awareness in consumer surveys.

### Metric interpretation

PAR is a measure of the effectiveness of *all actions taken along the customer's journey*, related to providing consumers aware of the brand with the desired information and facilitating brand purchase. The Purchase Activation Ratio is expected to range from 0 to 1, although values over 1 are also possible. Imagine a low-involvement product category and a private label with poor branding on its package. The penetration rate might be higher in such a case than the spontaneous brand awareness index. In other words, many brand buyers are, at least in this case, not aware of the brand they purchase. On the other hand, in the case of some prestigious brands, one can expect rather low values of PAR, because the percentage of consumers aware of the brand is much higher than those buying it (the apparent barrier to purchase is the price).

Low PAR (close to 0) is usually a signal of trouble for the brand owner. You can try to answer the question about the reasons for the low Purchase Activation Ratio, in the case of a particular brand:

1. In the case of FMCG, the problem may be the insufficient availability of the brand (see Section 3.1).
2. Consumers who became aware of a new brand, already have their favourite one in a product category. This argument may be valid for durable goods, much less in the case of FMCG, in which the risk of purchase is relatively lower (because of the lower price), and therefore the propensity to buy an unknown brand is usually higher.
3. In the case of durable goods, products of the new brand may seem attractive to consumers, but fears may result from a lack of confidence in accompanying services. For example, the smartphones of some new Chinese brands might not be available through official distribution channels in a particular

country, therefore consumers might be afraid of problems with after-sales service.

4. The purchase barrier in the case of a brand known to the consumer may be bad opinions about it. The questions then are: How bad were they? To what extent did they concern the critical attributes of the product? How many such critical opinions has the consumer heard? And how long ago was it?
5. Among those who do not buy a brand in a given period (e.g. a year) although they are aware of it, we may find consumers who had been buying the brand in the past but abandoned it a few years ago. In their case, the brand manager should try to determine: After what period of purchasing the brand was it abandoned? For what reason? How long ago did this happen? A closer look at the reasons for abandoning a brand or avoiding it because of negative opinions will allow you to take corrective action.

Suppose we know that the Purchase Activation Ratio is 0.5. It is obvious that to increase brand penetration by one percentage point, we need to increase spontaneous brand awareness by two percentage points. If, based on past experience, we are able to estimate the communication budget necessary to increase brand awareness by one percentage point and know the Purchase Activation Ratio, we are able to estimate the approximate cost of increasing the penetration rate by the desired value.

## 7.4. Brand contribution

It is worth noting that market share is one of the components of the so-called *brand contribution* to a company's profits (Best 2005), which is a metric that speaks louder to the chief financial officer (CFO) than brand awareness or the Net Promoter Score (NPS).

**Metric definition**

Brand contribution is a financial metric of a brand's share in its company's profits.

**Metric calculation**

Brand contribution = [market size * brand's market share * (revenue per customer – variable cost per customer)] – marketing expenses related to the brand (7.7)

**Example**

Let us assume that a market consists of 1 million customers, and a brand's market share in it is 15%. Yearly revenue per customer is 200 EUR and variable cost per customer is 140 EUR. The brand's yearly marketing budget is 2 million EUR. We can easily calculate the brand's contribution to its company's profits:

Brand contribution = [1,000,000 * 0.15 * (200 – 140] – 2,000,000 = 7,000,000 EUR

### Metric interpretation

If the brand owner wants to increase its brand's contribution to the company's profits, increasing market share is just one of the options in addition to

(1) increasing the market in which the brand competes (this would mean changing the market where a brand operates to another, more attractive category or geography);
(2) increasing revenue per customer;
(3) decreasing costs per customer;
(4) decreasing marketing expenses.

In some cases, companies try to achieve some of these goals simultaneously. There are some strategies (such as 'blue ocean') that try to mix activities targeted at increasing market share and customer revenues with lowering marketing expenses. Those are beyond the scope of this book, so interested readers should consult Kim and Mauborgne (2005).

### Metric limitations

Positive brand contribution proves that a given brand is profitable. Yet, it is impossible to tell how *effectively* the brand equity has been built, because the value of the metric largely depends on the size of the market. In the preceding case, if the market was half that size (0.5 million customers), and the marketing budget was cut by 50% (to 0.5 million EUR), the brand contribution would be just 4 million EUR (market share and margin being constant). On the other hand, if the market size was double the original one (2 million customers), even if relative marketing costs were 50% higher (6 million EUR), the brand contribution would increase to 12 million EUR (market share and margin being constant).

It is therefore impossible to compare the brand contributions of brands operating in different geographical markets, even in the same product category. Market size has such a strong impact on a metric's value that it distorts our perception of the effectiveness of a brand's strategy (see Table 7.6).

Brand contribution in the case of brand A is double that of brand B, even though brand B has double the market share and double the margin and a 25%

**TABLE 7.6** Hypothetical data for two brands in the same category but different geographical markets

| | *Brand A* | *Brand B* |
|---|---|---|
| Number of customers | 10,000,000 | 1,000,000 |
| Brand's market share | 10% | 20% |
| Revenue per customer (in EUR) | 200 | 200 |
| Variable cost per customer (in EUR) | 140 | 80 |
| Marketing expenses (in EUR) | 4,000,000 | 300,000 |
| Brand contribution (in EUR) | 56,000,000 | 23,700,000 |

lower marketing cost per customer than brand A. Yet, because brand A operates in a market that is 10 times larger, its brand contribution has to be higher.

Consequently, *every global brand* having, let's say, 500 million customers, no matter how low its market share is (say, just 2%), and how low the margin per customer it generates yearly (say, just 20 EUR), even in the case of a quite large marketing budget (say, 150 million EUR), would still present an *impressive contribution to the company's profits* (in that case it would be 50 million EUR).

Another problem with brand contribution is its misleading name – it suggests that the contribution comes from the impact of the brand alone. Yet, it is also the impact of a product/service and the benefits provided to customers. Even if the brand in a particular case was extremely 'weak' (having no impact whatsoever on the purchase decision), no-logo product, not supported by any marketing activities (therefore its budget is zero), when sold on a large market, for the price covering all costs, even if purchased by a small percentage of potential buyers, it would still generate a contribution to the company's profits, as can be seen below:

100,000,000 (number of customers) * 0.01 (market share of 1%) * 1 (yearly margin on a customer, in EUR) = 1,000,000 EUR

In large markets, you don't need a strong brand to have a positive brand contribution.

## 7.5 Brand's surplus margin

Another financial metric that might be used to prove the benefits of building a strong brand is the brand's surplus margin. It can be treated as a kind of test of a brand's health. A strong brand compared with weaker rivals should be more willingly bought; should have a higher profit margin; should have more effective marketing (each euro or dollar spent should bring better effects); should have higher customer retention rates, as well as a higher propensity to recommend the brand. A brand's surplus margin allows putting a financial value on all those advantages.

### Metric definition

*A brand's surplus margin* is the financial metric of the added value generated by a brand over a weak brand or no-logo offer. It is the current value of discounted[10] streams of surplus margin generated by a brand above the margin generated by a comparable weak brand or no-logo product, over a period of 5–10 years.

### Metric calculation

A brand's surplus margin calculation should be based on historic data (for a given brand) and some estimates (in the case of 'weak brands' or a no-logo offer). There are a few approaches to calculate the BSM. You will find them below (Formulas 7.8–7.10), together with examples.

1. When the margins and retention rates are known, the BSM can be calculated as

Brand's surplus margin = [(number of brand customers ⋆ brand margin ⋆ brand retention rate) : (1 + discount rate – brand retention rate)] – [(number of customers of a weak brand ⋆ margin of a weak brand ⋆ retention rate of a weak brand) : (1 + discount rate – retention rate of a weak brand)] (7.8)

**Example**

Let's say that a manager of a branded, national cable TV service has gathered data on margins, retention rates and the number of customers of its own company and a weak local competitor (Table 7.7).

In that case, the BSM equals: 62,222,222.22 – 4,952,380.95 = 57,269,841.27 EUR

2. When you have data on customer loyalty and the number and value of transactions per year, you can calculate the BSM as follows:

Brand's surplus margin = [(average value of a brand transaction – average brand transaction cost) ⋆ (number of brand transactions per year ⋆ number of years customers usually stay with the brand) – brand acquisition cost + (average brand acquisition cost ⋆ average brand reference rate)] ⋆ number of brand customers ⋆ adjustment factor – [(average value of a transaction of a weak brand – average transaction cost of a weak brand) ⋆ (number of transactions of a weak brand per year ⋆ number of years customers usually stay with the weak brand) – acquisition cost of a weak brand + (average acquisition cost of a weak brand ⋆ average reference rate of a weak brand)] ⋆ number of customers of a weak brand ⋆ adjustment factor (7.9)

where the 'adjustment factor' is the subjective estimate of changing customers' spending, and is above 1 if we expect it to grow, or below 1 if we think it is going to decrease over time.

In this case, in order to get data on the number of years that clients stay with the brand and the average number of visits per year, it pays to have loyalty programmes for customers. Also, businesses where customers are identified by name

**TABLE 7.7** Hypothetical data for two competing brands of a cable TV

| | *Our brand* | *'Weak brand'* |
|---|---|---|
| Number of customers | 100,000 | 20,000 |
| Brand margin (per year) in EUR | 210.00 | 160.00 |
| Yearly retention rate | 80% | 65% |
| Discount rate | 7% | 7% |
| Customers value | 62,222,222.22 | 4,952,380.95 |

(banks, insurance companies, car dealers, telecoms, etc.) can easily come up with those data.

**Example**

Suppose that a marketing manager of a small hotel chain has some data on customer retention and acquisition and their spending, both for a given chain and hotels of a 'weak brand'. Let's say that the latter metrics are in each case just 10% worse (see Table 7.8).

In that case, the BSM equals: 174,848,437.5 – 118,280,608.8 = 56,567,828.7 EUR.

3. Another formula is based on known costs and prices paid by customers:

Brand's surplus margin = sum for subsequent years [(price of a given brand paid in year n – brand's customer service costs in year *n*) / (1 – discount rate) $^n$] – acquisition costs in case of a given brand – sum for subsequent years [(price of a 'weak' brand paid in year *n* – weak brand's customer service costs in year *n*) / (1 – discount rate) $^n$] – acquisition costs in case of a weak brand (7.10)

where *n* is the period of time analyzed (somewhere between 5 and 10 years).

**Example**

Let's try to calculate the BSM (based on Formula 7.10) for a brand that five years ago had 100,000 customers and acquired 5,000 new ones in year *n* – 4, as a result of spending 200,000 EUR on marketing. In year *n* – 2, the brand manager

**TABLE 7.8** Hypothetical data for two competing hotels

| | *Our brand* | *'Weak brand'* |
|---|---|---|
| Average money spent per one visit (EUR) | 150 | 136 |
| Average cost to service one guest (EUR) | 75 | 68 |
| Average number of visits per year | 2.25 | 2.05 |
| Number of years the guest returns to the hotel | 7.5 | 6.8 |
| Acquisition cost (per new customer) (EUR) | 20 | 22 |
| Reference rate (number of guests referred by average customer) | 1.3 | 1.18 |
| Adjustment factor | 1.1 | 1.09 |
| Number of customers (per year) | 125,000 | 114,000 |
| Customers value | [(150 – 75) * (2.25*7.5) – 20 + (20 * 1.3)] * 125,000 * 1.1 = 174,848,437.5 | [(136 – 68) * (2.05 * 6.8) – 22 + (22 * 1.18)] * 114,000 * 1,09 = 118,280,608.8 |

decided to make another acquisition campaign, this time with a budget of 100,000 EUR. Thanks to the experience already gained, it has now been possible to attract proportionally more, i.e. 3,000 additional customers. Simultaneously, a programme was launched aimed at obtaining recommendations from already acquired customers. One free package was offered to brand customers who had recommended it to their friends (reference rates are shown in the Table 7.9). The percentage of retained customers each year is also shown in Table 7.9. The average customer buys three packages of a brand per year, for 15 EUR each and direct costs account for 65% of revenues (those are constant for the whole analyzed period). At the same time, the brand manager of the given brand has analyzed the data for a weaker competitor, offering much the same product. For analysis sake, let us assume that the weaker brand's metrics are just 10% worse than those of the given brand. What is the brand's surplus margin for a five-year period in this case?

In that case, the BSM equals: 7,710,492 – 3,637,520= 4,072,972 EUR.

Although the analyzed brand started five years ago with just 10% more customers than its weaker rival, because of slightly (10%) higher retention and reference rates, it has finished with 70% more customers after five years. Five years ago, the analyzed brand had revenues 37% higher than the weaker brand – today they are more than double the value of the 'weak brand'. A slightly higher consumption level (10%) and price (10%) made all the difference.

No wonder the cumulated discounted margin over just five years for the analyzed brand is more than double that of the weaker brand.

### Metric interpretation

A brand's surplus margin is *not* the financial value of the brand. It is the current value of discounted streams of surplus margin (above that delivered by a 'weak brand' or no-logo product), generated over the analyzed period (5–10 years) by a given brand. In other words, it eliminates the impact of the benefits provided by the product, and includes only the brand's strengths such as customer loyalty and their predisposition to recommend the brand; its price premium; and higher communication effectiveness.

Of course, the higher the value of the BSM, the better. For a brand manager who would like to compare his/her own brand's surplus margin with, for example, the market leader, this short exercise may prove to be difficult or even impossible to accomplish because of the lack of data. But it is always possible to compare the BSM for the same brand over time, with changes to its marketing strategy. An increase in the BSM is indisputable proof of an increase in the brand's strength.

### Metric limitations

Brand owners, especially those whose business model entails supplying an identified customer, would have no problem gathering all the data to calculate the gross margin of their brands. As for the reference value of the data on a so-called 'weak brand' or 'no-logo offer', this has to be estimated. A so-called 'opinionated guess' is still a guess. Unfortunately, even small differences in those

**TABLE 7.9** Hypothetical data for two competing brands

| | *Year n – 4* | | *Year n – 3* | | *Year n – 2* | | *Year n – 1* | | *Year n* | |
|---|---|---|---|---|---|---|---|---|---|---|
| | *Brand* | *Weak* | *Brand* | *Weak* | *Brand* | *Weak* | *Brand* | *Weak* | *Brand* | *Weak* |
| Number of newly acquired customers | 5,000 | 4,500 | XXXXXX | XXXXXX | 3,000 | 2,700 | XXXXXX | XXXXXX | XXXXXX | XXXXXX |
| Retention rate (%) | 90 | 81 | 90 | 81 | 92 | 83 | 92 | 83 | 92 | 83 |
| Retained customers (from previous year) | 100,000 | 90,000 | 94,500 | 76,545 | 86,940 | 63,532,35 | 86,882,04 | 57,446,79 | 83,927,92 | 49,826,56 |
| Reference rate (%) | 0 | 0 | 0 | 0 | 5 | 4.5 | 5 | 4.5 | 5 | 4.5 |
| Referential customers | 0 | 0 | 0 | 0 | 4,497 | 2,980,456 | 4,344,102 | 2,585,106 | 4,196,396 | 2,242,195 |
| Total number of customers (rounded) | 105,000 | 94,500 | 94,500 | 76,545 | 94,437 | 69,213 | 91,226 | 60,032 | 88,124 | 52,069 |
| Number of packages consumed yearly | 3 | 2.7 | The same | | | | | | | |
| Price paid | 15 | 13.5 | The same | | | | | | | |
| Revenues of customers: | | | | | | | | | | |
| Paying full price | 4,725,000 | 3,444,525 | 4,252,500 | 2,790,065 | 4,047,300 | 2,414,169 | 3,909,692 | 2,093,935 | 3,776,756 | 1,816,178 |
| With bonus | 0 | 0 | 0 | 0 | 134,910 | 68,401,46 | 130,323,1 | 59,328,17 | 125,891,9 | 51,458,38 |
| Total revenues | 4,725,000 | 3,444,525 | 4,252,500 | 2,790,065 | 4,182,210 | 2,482,571 | 4,040,015 | 2,153,264 | 3,902,648 | 1,867,636 |
| Costs: | | | | | | | | | | |
| Acquisition | 200,000 | 200,000 | XXXXXX | XXXXXX | 100,000 | 100,000 | XXXXXX | XXXXXX | XXXXXX | XXXXXX |
| Direct (%) | 65 | 71.5 | the same | | | | | | | |
| Direct (EUR) | 3,071,250 | 2,462,835 | 2,764,125 | 1,994,897 | 2,762,282 | 1,803,812 | 2,668,361 | 1,564,539 | 2,577,627 | 1,357,009 |
| Total | 3,271,250 | 2,662,835 | 2,764,125 | 1,994,897 | 2,862,282 | 1,903,812 | 2,668,361 | 1,564,539 | 2,577,627 | 1,357,009 |
| Gross margin | 1,453,750 | 7,816,896 | 1,488,375 | 7,951,686 | 1,319,928 | 578,758,7 | 1,371,654 | 588,724,7 | 1,325,021 | 510,627,2 |
| Discount rate $(1 + 0.05)^n$ | 1,2155 | 1,2155 | 1,157,625 | 1,157,625 | 1,1025 | 1,1025 | 1.05 | 1,05 | 1 | 1 |
| Discounted margin | 1,767,033 | 9,501,437 | 1,722,980 | 920,507 | 1,455,220 | 638,081,5 | 1,440,237 | 618160,9 | 1,325,021 | 510,627,2 |
| Cumulated discounted margin | 1,767,033 | 9,501,437 | 3,490,013 | 1,870,651 | 4,945,234 | 2,508,732 | 6,385,471 | 3,126,893 | 7,710,492 | 3,637,520 |

estimates with regard to actual values might have a considerable impact on the surplus margin.

Consider what would happen with the BSM if, in able 7.9, just the retention rate and the reference rate for a 'weak brand' were only two percentage points lower (see Table 7.10).

In that case, the BSM equals: 7,710,492 – 3,507,685 = 4,202,807 EUR.

The difference is nearly 130,000 EUR. And that is because our estimates for just two metrics were two percentage points off! Just imagine what would happen if we wrongly estimated the number of customers or costs. Those might have an enormous impact on a brand's surplus margin.

Another problem is the time horizon for calculations of the BSM. Of course, the longer the time period over which the surplus margin is calculated, the higher the BSM value. Therefore, if the BSM is used in negotiations with the CFO over the marketing budget supporting the brand, the CMO might be tempted to calculate the BSM over 10 years or an even longer period. However, estimating metrics for an imagined 'weak brand' or no-logo offer is still more complicated, if you go back 10 years or more. As to the time horizon, 5–10 years seems to be a reasonable compromise.

### Case

*Direct Line Group (DLG) is a British insurance company that owns a few brands – Direct Line, Green Flag, Churchill and Privilege among them. Privilege was launched in 1994 and sometime between 2007 and 2009 its above-the-line marketing support was strongly reduced. As a result, its spontaneous awareness dropped from around 7% to just 3%. Churchill, on the other hand, has enjoyed much higher communication spending. Although both brands were supported by the same contact centres and claims handlers and enjoyed similar satisfaction and complaints rates, various metrics differed between the two brands (see Table 7.11).*

*One may safely take Privilege as a 'weak' or 'non brand', with its equity being rather low (although not non-existent).*

## Recommendations for brand managers

1. Analyzing just the sales of a brand, you cannot be sure whether it is doing great or not. You have to take market share into account. And not just the value for a given year, but also a year or two before, and the market share of your strongest competitor.
2. But even an exhaustive analysis of your brand's market share won't tell you what to do in order to increase it. It is necessary to dig deeper into brand penetration, its share of wallet, weighted distribution and share-in-shops-handling. For details, consult Table 7.4 and Chapters 3 and 5.
3. You can evaluate the effectiveness of marketing activities along the customer's journey, from the 'awareness' to the 'purchase' stage, by using the Purchase Activation Ratio. In the majority of cases, it should be well above 0, and values over 1 are a sign of trouble with the brand.

**TABLE 7.10** Changes in revenues and costs if retention and reference rates for a weaker brand were two percentage points lower

| | *Year* n – 4 | | *Year* n – 3 | | *Year* n – 2 | | *Year* n – 1 | | *Year* n | |
|---|---|---|---|---|---|---|---|---|---|---|
| | *Brand* | *Weak* | *Brand* | *Weak* | *Brand* | *Weak* | *Brand* | *Weak* | *Brand* | *Weak* |
| Number of newly acquired customers | 5,000 | 4,500 | XXXXXX | XXXXXX | 3,000 | 2,700 | XXXXXX | XXXXXX | XXXXXX | XXXXXX |
| Retention rate (%) | 90 | 79 | 90 | 79 | 92 | 81 | 92 | 81 | 92 | 81 |
| Retained customers (from previous year) | 100,000 | 90,000 | 94,500 | 74,655 | 86,940 | 60,470,55 | 86,882,04 | 50,260,5 | 83,927,92 | 41,728,77 |
| Reference rate (%) | 0 | 0 | 0 | 0 | 5 | 2.5 | 5 | 2.5 | 5 | 2.5 |
| Referential customers | 0 | 0 | 0 | 0 | 4,497 | 1,579,264 | 4,344,102 | 1,256,513 | 4,196,396 | 1,043,219 |
| Total number of customers (rounded) | 105,000 | 94,500 | 94,500 | 74,655 | 94,437 | 62,050 | 91,226 | 51,517 | 88,124 | 42,772 |
| Number of packages consumed yearly | 3 | 2.7 | The same | | | | | | | |
| Price paid | 15 | 13.5 | The same | | | | | | | |
| Revenues of customers: | | | | | | | | | | |
| Paying full price | 4,725,000 | 3,444,525 | 4,252,500 | 2,721,175 | 4,047,300 | 2,302,567 | 3,909,692 | 1,831,995 | 3,776,756 | 1,521,014 |
| With bonus | 0 | 0 | 0 | 0 | 134,910 | 36,244,1 | 130,323,1 | 28,836,96 | 125,891,9 | 23,941,88 |
| Total revenues | 4,725,000 | 3,444,525 | 4,252,500 | 2,721,175 | 4,182,210 | 2,338,811 | 4,040,015 | 1,860,832 | 3,902,648 | 1,544,956 |
| Costs: | | | | | | | | | | |
| Acquisition | 200,000 | 200,000 | XXXXXX | XXXXXX | 100,000 | 100000 | XXXXXX | XXXXXX | XXXXXX | XXXXXX |
| Direct (%) | 65 | 71.5 | The same | | | | | | | |
| Direct (EUR) | 3,071,250 | 2,462,835 | 2,764,125 | 1,945,640 | 2762,282 | 1617132 | 2668361 | 1342623 | 2577627 | 1,114,713 |
| Total | 3,271,250 | 2,662,835 | 2,764,125 | 1,945,640 | 2,862,282 | 1717132 | 2668361 | 1342623 | 2577627 | 1,114,713 |
| Gross margin | 1,453,750 | 781,689,6 | 1,488,375 | 775,534,8 | 1,319,928 | 621679,1 | 1371654 | 518209 | 1325021 | 430,242,4 |
| Discount rate $(1 + 0.05)^n$ | 1,2155 | 1,2155 | 1,157625 | 1,157625 | 1,1025 | 1,1025 | 1,05 | 1,05 | 1 | 1 |
| Discounted margin | 1,767,033 | 950,143,7 | 1,722,980 | 897,778,5 | 1,455,220 | 685401,2 | 1440237 | 544119,5 | 1325021 | 430,242,4 |
| Cumulated discounted margin | 1,767,033 | 950,143,7 | 3,490,013 | 1,847,922 | 4,945,234 | 2,533,323 | 6385471 | 3077443 | 7710492 | 3,507,685 |

**TABLE 7.11** Brand metrics for Churchill and Privilege in 2016

| | *Churchill* | *Privilege* |
|---|---|---|
| Ad spend in 2008–2016 (in GBP million) | 120.7 | 4.6 |
| Spontaneous awareness (%) | 38 | 3 |
| Prompted awareness (%) | 86 | 41 |
| Brand consideration (%) | 19 | 2 |
| Trustworthiness (%) | 35 | 24 |
| Brand preference (%) at different price levels: | | |
| Same prices | 83 | 17 |
| Price of a given brand lower than rival by 10–19 GBP | 93 | 67 |
| Price of a given brand lower than rival by 20–29 GBP | 96 | 81 |
| Price of a given brand lower than rival by 30–39 GBP | 98 | 88 |
| Click-through rate when brand is ranked first | 12.1 | 9.4 |
| Click-through rate when brand is ranked second | 5.7 | 2.7 |
| Click-through rate when brand is ranked third | 2.9 | 1.4 |

Source: Bratton et al. (2018).

4. If as a marketer you expect your voice to be heard at executive meetings, try to prove the financial value of your brand. Using metrics such as brand contribution or a brand's surplus margin might do wonders. They might not prompt any marketing tricks but will substantiate your claims for an increased brand budget.

## Questions

1. Why is analyzing sales alone not enough to diagnose a brand's health?
2. What mistakes can be made when measuring market share?
3. Which brand metric explains the varying levels of market shares of different brands?
4. Let's say that the Purchase Activation Ratio is 0.33. From past experience, we know that raising brand awareness by one percentage point costs us circa 50,000 EUR. How much must we spend to increase the brand's penetration from 19.5% to 20%?
5. Why is the surplus margin of a strong brand higher than in the case of a weaker brand (competing in the same market)?

## Notes

1 If we extend the time period for which the market share is analyzed (e.g. from a quarter to six months or from six months to a year), it should be noted that the penetration rate (see Formula 7.2) will increase although non-linearly. In other words, a brand's annual penetration will be less than four times its quarterly penetration. On the other hand, the share of wallet will decrease as the analysis period extends. For the quarter, it will be higher than for the whole year. When we multiply the penetration rate by the brand's share of wallet and get its market share, we understand that it is quite

stable over time when the period of analysis is extended. In other words, market share does not depend on the length of the period for which it is calculated: the annual and semi-annual will be about the same.

2 The Brand Price Index informs about the relation of the retail price of a brand to the average retail price of all brands in a product category, so it is calculated as
Brand Price Index = 100 * average retail price of a brand : average retail price of all brands in a category
The brand that has a higher value than the volume market share sells its products at prices higher than the average in a product category (and vice versa). In 2016, the price index of Guinness in Great Britain was 143 (Gallery and Sor 2016), which means that this brand was 43% more expensive than the average price of beer in the UK. Both prestigious and very cheap brands can have volume market shares significantly different from value shares.

3 The heavy usage index is calculated as follows:
Heavy usage index = number of product packages purchased by average brand buyer : number of product packages purchased by average category buyer
The heavy usage index oscillates around a value of 1. In practice, in the case of brands with the largest market shares, its value is slightly above 1 (around 1.1), while the vast majority of brands have heavy usage indices slightly below 1 (around 0.9–0.95). The heavy usage index tells us if brand buyers are heavy users of a category. There are no reasons to assume that just buyers of a particular brand of coffee, yogurt or shampoo should buy this product (note: the product, not the brand!) in more (or less) quantities than the average category buyer. Every year, beer drinkers buying brand X purchase much the same amount of beer cans or bottles as buyers of brand Y or Z. The name of that metric in English perfectly reflects its essence, because exceeding the value of 1 for a given brand is possible only when it has an unusually high percentage of heavy users of the product.

4 For example, I've recorded my own smartphone purchases from the last 10 years (of course, you can take a shorter period, e.g. five years, but then the number of purchases will be smaller, and therefore the precision of determining the share of wallet lower), coming up with the following collection of brands (from the oldest): Nokia, Samsung, HTC, Sony, Huawei, LG, Lenovo, Huawei, Samsung, Meizu, Huawei, Honor, LG, Honor, Xiaomi and Xiaomi. It follows that the share of my wallet (for example) of Samsung brand is 100 * 2/16 = 12.5% (if we included brands from the last five years the score for Samsung would be slightly lower: 100 * 1/10 = 10%). The same calculations need to be done on a larger scale (let's say, 1,000 smartphone users). Now, Samsung's brand penetration in the smartphone market for a period of 10 years (what percentage of smartphones buyers from the last 10 years bought at least one product of this brand) and what is its heavy usage index (i.e. the ratio of the number of smartphones bought in the last 10 years by users who purchased a Samsung phone at least once, divided by the average number of smartphone purchases for an average buyer) need to be established. In the case of durable goods, *it should not be assumed that the heavy usage index for each brand will be equal to 1*, because there is a segment of buyers who prefer cheaper brands, focused more on frequent replacement of the device due to their physical wear-out or the feeling that by doing so, the device at their disposal offers all the latest gimmicks. As you can see, those calculations are complicated to perform, yet the formula for market share is identical.

5 The formula comes from the following transformations:
Brand's market share = brand's sales : total category sales = brand's sales : total category sales * (category sales in shops handling the brand : category sales in shops handling the brand) = (brand's sales : category sales in shops handling the brand) * (category sales in shops handling the brand : total category sales) = brand's share-in-shops-handling * weighted distribution

6 The formula comes from the following transformations:

Retailer's X value market share = retailer's X sales : total sales of a category = (number of transactions in retailer's X stores * average receipt in retailer's X stores ) : (number of transactions in stores of a particular trade * average receipt in stores of a particular trade) = (number of customers of retailer X * average number of visits in stores X per customer * average receipt in retailer's X stores) : (number of customers in stores of a particular trade * average number of visits in stores of a particular trade * average receipt in stores of a particular trade) = (number of customers of retailer X : number of customers in stores of a particular trade) * (average number of visits in stores X per customer : average number of visits in stores of a particular trade) * (average receipt in retailer's X stores : average receipt in stores of a particular trade) = penetration rate * relative frequency of visits * relative receipt

7 For example, in 2017 the German discounter Aldi was visited by an average British customer 19.8 times (Hawkins and Peate 2018). At that time, Aldi's market share value in the UK was 6.8% (Gregory and Parnum 2020). Over the next two years, it had increased to 7.9% (Peate and Koropisz 2020).

8 Interestingly, it not only applies to consumer goods, but also to TV series. Less popular TV series not only have a smaller (than popular shows) audience, but subsequent episodes of the season are watched by a smaller percentage of viewers (Ehrenberg et al. 1998).

9 That does not necessarily mean an increase in the number of stores in which it is sold. It is rather a question of choosing stores of great importance for a given category (see also Section 3.1). For now, brand Y is unavailable in the vast majority of important stores.

10 The discount rate reflects the cost of invested capital, and takes into account inflation, return on risk-free investment and business risk.

## Literature


Armstrong J.S., Green K.C. 2007, Competitor-oriented Objectives: The Myth of Market Share, *International Journal of Business*, 12(1), pp. 115–134.

Bendle N.T., Bagga Ch.K., 2016, The Metrics That Marketers Muddle, *MIT Sloan Management Review*, Spring, pp. 73–81.

Bendle N.T., Farris P.W., Pfeifer Ph.E., Reibstein D.J., 2016, *Marketing Metrics: The Manager's Guide to Measuring Marketing Performance*, Third Edition, Pearson Education, Upper Saddle River.

Best R.J., 2005, *Market-based Management*, Pearson Prentice Hall, Upper Saddle River.

Binet L., Field P., 2007, *Marketing in the Era of Accountability: Identifying the Marketing Practices and Metrics That Truly Increase Profitability*, World Advertising Research Center, Henley-on-Thames.

Bratton C., Constantine A., Pietersma N., 2016, Direct Line: We Solve Problems, in: *Advertising Works 23: Proving the Payback on Marketing Investment*, ed. B. Angear, Institute of Practitioners in Advertising + WARC, London, pp. 139–164.

Bratton C., Constantine A., Pietersma N., 2018, Direct Line Group: They Went Short. We Went Long, in: *Advertising Works 24: Proving the Payback on Marketing Investment*, ed. N. Godber, Institute of Practitioners in Advertising + WARC, London, pp.157–184.

Butler S., 2020, Crazy Golf on the First Floor ? UK's Department Stores Face Radical Remake, *The Guardian*, 6 December.

Clouder J., 2018, How Lidl Grew a Lot, in: *Advertising Works 24: Proving the Payback on Marketing Investment*, ed. N. Godber, Institute of Practitioners in Advertising + WARC, London, pp. 227–252.

*Coccolino*, 2020, *Czolowe marki konsumenckie i biznesowe w Polsce*, Superbrands Polska, Warszawa, pp. 32–33.

Corsjtens M, Lal R., 2000, Building Store Loyalty Through Store Brands, *Journal of Marketing Research*, August, pp. 281–291, doi: 10.1509/jmkr.37.3.281.18781.

Courtney R., Herbert Ch., Harwood S., 2018, Suzuki Saturdays, in: *Advertising Works 24: Proving the Payback on Marketing Investment*, ed. N. Godber, Institute of Practitioners in Advertising + WARC, London, pp. 283–304.

Davis J.A., 2018, *Measuring Marketing – The 100+ Essential Metrics Every Marketer Needs*, Third Edition, Walter de Gruyter Inc, Boston.

Dekimpe M.G., Hanssens D.M., 1995, Empirical Generalizations About Market Evolution and Stationarity, *Marketing Science*, 14(3) (Part 2 of 2), pp.109–121, doi: 10.1287/mksc.14.3.G109.

East R., Wright M., Vanhuele M., 2008, *Consumer Behaviour: Applications in Marketing*, SAGE, Los Angeles.

Ehrenberg A.S.C., Goodhardt G.J., Barwise T.P., 1990, Double Jeopardy Revisited, *Journal of Marketing*, 54(3), pp. 82–91 doi: 10.2307/1251818.

Gallery R., Sor L., 2016, Guinness: An Effectiveness Story Made of More, in: *Advertising Works 23: Proving the Payback on Marketing Investment*, ed. B. Angear, Institute of Practitioners in Advertising + WARC, London, pp. 165–208.

Gregory S., Parnum J., 2020, From Running Shops to Serving Customers: The Tesco Turnaround Story, in: *Advertising Works 25: Proving the Payback on Marketing Investment*, ed. S. Unerman, Institute of Practitioners in Advertising + WARC by Ascential, London, pp. 47–86.

Hawkins D., Peate J., 2018, Shop. Eat. Repeat. How a Bold Repositioning Campaign Restored Aldi to Record Growth, in: *Advertising Works 24: Proving the Payback on Marketing Investment*, ed. N. Godber, Institute of Practitioners in Advertising + WARC, London, pp. 390–391.

IDC, 2020, *Smartphone Market Share*, 22 June, www.idc.com/promo/smartphone-market-share/vendor [access: 17.12.2020].

Jones J.Ph., Slater J.S., 2003, *What's In a Name? Advertising and the Concept of Brands*, M.E. Sharpe, London.

Kim W.Ch., Mauborgne R., 2005, *Blue Ocean Strategy: How to Create Uncontested Market Space and Make the Competition Irrelevant*, Harvard Business School Press, Boston.

Kotler Ph., 1974, Atmosferics as a Marketing Tool, *Journal of Retailing*, 49(4), pp. 48–64.

Kotler Ph., Kartajaya H., Setiawan I., 2017, *Marketing 4.0: Moving from Traditional to Digital*, John Wiley & Sons, Hoboken, NJ.

Lahart J., 2020, The Department Store of the Future Will Look a Lot Like the Past, *Wall Street Journal*, 17 January.

Lion W., 2018, Audi UK: Beauty and Brains: How We Supercharged the Audi Premium 2015-2018, in: *Advertising Works 24: Proving the Payback on Marketing Investment*, ed. N. Godber, Institute of Practitioners in Advertising + WARC, London, pp. 45–82.

Meyer Z., 2020, Prime Numbers, *Fast Company*, Winter.

Parfitt J.H., Collins B.J.K., 1968, Use of Consumer Panels for Brand-Share Prediction, *Journal of Marketing Research*, 5(2), pp. 131–145, doi: 10.1177/002224376800500201.

Paynter B., 2019, Chobani Sows Its Oats, *Fast Company*, Winter, December–January/February.

Peate J., Koropisz M., 2020, Aldi 2010–2019: How Taking an Alternative Path Took Aldi from Shame to Prime, in: *Advertising Works 25: Proving the Payback on Marketing Investment*, ed. S. Unerman, Institute of Practitioners in Advertising + WARC by Ascential, London, pp. 254–255.

Rego L.L., Morgan N.A., Fornell C., 2013, Reexamining the Market Share–Customer Satisfaction Relationship, *Journal of Marketing*, 77(September), pp. 1–20, doi: 10.2307/23487420.

Ringen J., 2018, Nike Has a New Digital Playbook – and Is Starts With Sneakerheads, *Fast Company*, May.

Sharp B., 2017, *Marketing: Theory, Evidence, Practice*, Oxford University Press, Melbourne.

Singh J., Wright M., 2016, New Brands: Performance and Measurement, in: *The Routledge Companion to Contemporary Brand Management*, ed. F. Dall'Olmo Riley, J. Singh, Ch. Blankson, Routledge, London, pp. 186–197.

Stone M., 2020, Department Stores Are Considering Radical Changes to Stay a Float, and They May Soon Look Unrecognizable, Analysts Say, *Business Insider*, 5 August.

Stoney L., 2018, Guinness: 'Made of More' 2012–2018, in: *Advertising Works 24: Proving the Payback on Marketing Investment*, ed. N. Godber, Institute of Practitioners in Advertising + WARC, London, pp. 185–226.

Stoney L., Mawdsley C., 2020, Guinness 'Made of More' 2012–2019: Consistency x Creativity, in: *Advertising Works 25: Proving the Payback on Marketing Investment*, ed. S. Unerman, Institute of Practitioners in Advertising + WARC by Ascential, London, pp. 147–196.

'Storm in a Coffee Cup', 2019, *The Economist*, 23 February.

Szymanski D.M., Bharadwaj S.G., Varadarajan P.R., 1993, An Analysis of the Market Share-Profitability Relationship, *Journal of Marketing*, 57(3), pp. 1–18, doi: 10.1177/002224299305700301.

Wood Ch., 2020, John Lewis: An Amazing Decade, in: *Advertising Works 25: Proving the Payback on Marketing Investment*, ed. S. Unerman, Institute of Practitioners in Advertising + WARC by Ascential, London, pp. 197–237.

# EPILOGUE

'35 metrics! Does that mean that I have to analyze all of them?' Of course not.

First of all, the possibility of obtaining all relevant data for calculating a particular metric varies greatly. In some cases, I've tried to show possible problems in obtaining relevant data and, if available, have suggested alternative formulas to bypass those obstacles. Nevertheless, sometimes the cost of providing the necessary data might be prohibitive and the value that a specific metric delivers lower than the cost involved.

Secondly, the informative benefits of different metrics relating to the same stage of a customer's journey vary. For example, top-of-the-mind awareness says much more than prompted awareness. So if you have the former, do you really need the latter? What's more, some metrics can be reasonably inferred from others. If we have a brand with a high market share and high penetration, one can almost certainly assume that it also has a positive image (brand rates favourably in all key dimensions) and we can quite easily calculate its share of wallet. Even if market leaders might lose to some smaller competitors on a particular image dimension (each brand will have some weaknesses), the question arises whether it happens in areas that are really important for customers.

Thirdly, some metrics are useful in certain industries and business models, while in others they cannot be calculated at all, or their calculation is pointless (such as sentiment analysis in the case of a mundane or B2B products, or numeric distribution in the case of fashion brands offered in own stores only).

One has to agree with Bendle et al. (2016) that no single metric exists that tells the whole story about a brand. The same limitation applies to the evaluation of human health – no single measure (nor blood pressure nor heart rate) can reliably assess the overall health of an individual. Therefore, it may turn out that choosing a few, maybe *6 to 10* (certainly not 35) metrics, in the majority of cases is enough to get a reasonably complete picture of a brand's health. It is best to

DOI: 10.4324/9781003167235-8

| | Awareness | Consideration | Purchase | Satisfaction | Engagement | Advocacy |
|---|---|---|---|---|---|---|
| Preferable | Top-of-the mind awareness<br>Spontaneous awareness | Brand consideration<br>Brand preference | Weighted distribution<br>Share-in-shops handling<br>Penetration rate<br>Trial purchase (new brands) | Weighted satisfaction index | Share-of-wallet<br>Repeat purchase rate (new brands)<br>Retention rate (contract/ subscription and 'big ticket' items like cars) | Brand Advocacy Index |
| To consider | Aided awareness | Brand in Top3<br>Brand purchase intention | Numeric distribution | Customer Satisfaction Index<br>Net Promoter Score | Customer Loyalty Ratio<br>Sole brand users | Sentiment analysis<br>Brand Advocacy Ratio |

**FIGURE E.1** Metrics suggested for each stage of a customer's journey.

select them starting from a broader set of metrics, observed for some time to find out which of them had most accurately predicted in the past subsequent changes in the market position of the brand. Of course, one cannot be certain that metrics that had the greatest predictive capacity in the past maintain it in the future. But at least, the list of metrics is not purely intuitive. See Figure E.1 for suggestions about metrics that might be the most informative and the easiest to procure. Add to those metrics also market share and you will have a good starting point to build your own brand health scoreboard.

In the end, you should remember a few issues.

First of all, the metrics must refer to your company's strategy. Do we focus on gaining as many customers as possible or do we concentrate on maximizing the brand's share of wallet? As an experienced consultant, Tim Ambler (2003) aptly suggests that it makes no sense to choose as many metrics as possible, hoping that their analysis will uncover an optimal strategy for a brand. It is the current strategy that should guide our choice of metrics, not the other way around. You should use brand metrics not only to assess past marketing activities related to the brand but also to suggest future goals and tools for achieving them. Therefore, they must be relevant to the brand and provide the basis for making decisions that support its growth (Eechambadi 2005).

Secondly, the analysis of metrics should always be in relation to competitors. No value of spontaneous awareness, penetration, Net Promoter Score (NPS) or weighted distribution is in itself 'satisfactory' or 'too low', if we do not compare them to the metrics of competitors. We must also remember about the analysis of trends in metrics and not to draw definitive conclusions from a metric calculated for one point in time. The answer to the question of whether to be satisfied with 30% spontaneous awareness, 10% penetration and 40% weighted distribution depends on how those metrics changed in the previous periods: are they rising or falling or have they stabilized? We should not expect a full picture of a brand's health after a one-time effort to calculate a few metrics.

Thirdly, relative changes in metrics should not obscure their inherent importance. An increase in market share of just 0.2 percentage points (e.g. from 8.5% to 8.7%) on paper looks modest, compared with an increase in the number of brand followers from, say, 400,000–500,000. Yet, it is market share, and not necessarily the number of brand fans that is linked with business success.

Next, we should remember that impressive gains in metrics are more likely in the case of new, small brands than market leaders. The Institute of Practitioners in Advertising (IPA) databank (Binet and Field 2007) shows, for example, that improvements in awareness are more common for new brand launches and small brands. The same applies to penetration growth or market share gains. Growth rates for 'old' brands are lower than for 'new' ones, and in their case marketing should shift from short-term acquisition to long-term retention. Also in the case of new categories, brand metrics are more responsive than the more mature ones. Metrics should always be analyzed in market contexts, taking into consideration the product category, competitors and the brand's history.

Last but not least, the metrics presented in this book should not be used to evaluate specific marketing activity, but rather to assess the overall condition or strength of a brand. Of course, the impact of marketing activities, especially in the long term, is included in the metrics' scores. But let's not treat the increase in brand awareness as proof of the effectiveness of the last advertising campaign, nor the increase in the penetration rate as dependent solely on the last consumer promotion we ran.

One cannot reasonably expect to paint a complete picture of a brand using only brand metrics. But without them, a verbal account reporting a brand's health, no matter how long, would miss the point even more. Numbers do not substitute for creativity and intuition, but beware of brand strategies, where brand metrics are few and far between. You might find a lot of inspiration in numbers if they are well understood and used sensibly.

## Literature

Amber T., 2003, *Marketing and the Bottom Line*, Prentice Hall – Financial Times, London.

Bendle N.T., Farris P.W., Pfeifer Ph. E., Reibstein D.J., 2016, *Marketing Metrics: The Manager's Guide to Measuring Marketing Performance*, Third Edition, Pearson Education, Upper Saddle River.

Binet L., Field P., 2007, *Marketing in the Era of Accountability: Identifying the Marketing Practices and Metrics That Truly Increase Profitability*, World Advertising Research Center, Henley-on-Thames.

Eechambadi N., 2005, *High Performance Marketing: Bringing Method to the Madness of Marketing*, Dearborn Trade Publishing, Chicago.

# APPENDIX 1

## How does our brain operate?

Our brain consists of three separate parts, each with different cellular structures and functions (Renvoisé and Morin 2007; Pradeep 2010; van Praet 2012; Parry 2013; Waytz and Mason 2013; Magrini 2017).

The central and oldest part of the brain is sometimes referred to as the *reptile brain* because similar structures exist today in the brains of reptiles. The *old* or *first brain* is the part of the brain that is formed first in the human embryo. The reptile brain works independently of conscious will or thinking, in the 24/7 mode, and is a hotbed of primal instincts. For thousands of years, the brain has managed the life activities that condition the survival of organisms: breathing, heart rate and body temperature; over 40 different unconditional reflexes (such as coughing, sneezing, yawning and vomiting); and motor coordination. The reptile brain does not have the ability to learn by experience. It automatically repeats certain behavioural patterns that are impulsive, sometimes even obsessive or ritual. Van Praet (2012) describes those unconscious, primal instincts as survival, safety, security, sustenance, sex and status. It was the natural selection process that made those 6S necessary for survival.

Language is not the domain of the reptile brain, which means that a too complicated message expressed in words does not allow it to make a quick decision. The reptile brain mainly interprets visual stimuli, perhaps because the optic nerve is directly connected to it, and therefore works 40 times faster than the auditory nerve. Besides, over a third of the brain is involved in visual stimuli processing. Anything that is easily recognizable, familiar, friendly and unchanging can help in the operations of the old brain. The reptile brain is lazy and energy-consuming. The whole brain is only 2%–3% of body mass, but while at rest, it absorbs as much as one-fourth of the energy that the whole organism consumes. For comparison, in the case of monkeys, it is only 8% (Harari 2015). Therefore, whenever possible, the reptile brain does not engage the new brain if the decision can be made instinctively.

The reptile brain often plays a significant role in the decision-making process, because it determines which sensory stimuli (and every second our body is exposed to 11 million bits of information, from which we consciously process only 40) reaches the so-called new brain. And it is the reptile brain that accepts decisions taken by reason. The old brain copes badly with tasks that take too much time; with excess stimuli and with stimuli that distract or do not fit the context. Instead, it reacts strongly to any contrast, especially between what has been until then and what suddenly happened. The reptile brain is able to constantly monitor the environment for any changes that could threaten the organism. The contrast between what is new and what is old and what is fast and what is slow makes it easier to take quick, usually correct decisions. When we notice a speeding car approaching us, there is no time for long deliberations on how to behave.

So, these are primary instincts that are responsible for taking many actions, not rational reasoning. Those instincts, embedded in cultural forces, motivate us to take a particular action. As a result of evolution, our rational mind has learned to perform many functions more efficiently, but it has not changed the reasons why we undertake specific activities. So, it is not the reason that initiates our actions. This does not mean, of course, that we are totally controlled by our instincts and that each of us, in order to gain status or sustenance, is capable of the same deeds. Much depends on the emotional state of the individual and his/her personal history and cultural background (Calne 2010).

Around the reptile brain is a structure called the *middle brain* (or *emotional* brain; it has developed together with the appearance of mammals), which is responsible for supporting memory, motivation, the processing of emotions and instinctive reactions. It directs our attention to selected objects; it is responsible for interpersonal relationships, or our relationships with brands, as well as our memories of them. In the centre of the middle brain is the amygdala,[1] where memories are tagged by emotions. As a result of an experience with a brand, this part of the brain tags it emotionally. The amygdala together with the hippocampus is involved in the learning process, referred to as the association memory. The hippocampus is responsible for remembering a brand name and the shape or colour of the packaging, while the amygdala marks those memories with positive or negative emotions. When the brand is seen again, the brain uses those tags, treating them as a shortcut for evoking emotions: fear, happiness, excitement, etc. Thanks to this, when exposed to specific external stimuli, the brain accelerates the decision-making process. The use of emotional tags is meant to replace complex and exhausting analysis.

Comparing the role of emotions with reason, we should stress that emotions lead us to act, while reason leads to conclusions. Emotions crave satisfaction which means that they stimulate us either to seek psychological rewards (things that make us feel good) or to avoid psychological punishments (things that make us feel bad). Reason, on the other hand, has no craving, no demand for satisfaction. In the process of evolution, those mental rewards and punishments have been encoded into our memory, guaranteeing the survival of the individual. When we re-experience the stimulus or even the mental image of the event or brand, we tend to rekindle mental rewards or punishments (Calne 2010). Emotions are therefore necessary in the decision-making process, especially when one has limited information resources. In this case, the role of intuition cannot be overestimated (Magrini 2017).

Referring to brands, DePlessis (2011) called the set of emotional associations 'brand soma'. Those are the feelings resulting from emotions that a brand provided in the past, which accompany the interpretation of brand-related stimuli, reaching from the limbic system to the frontal lobes in the brain. They are helpful in making consumer choices and therefore a very important question for customers should be: 'how would you feel using brand X?'.

The *new brain* (cerebral cortex) develops fully around the age of 25–30 years and is a distinguishing feature of humans and other primates. It accounts for up to 90% of the total weight of the brain. It is responsible for conscious will; rational information processing; higher skills such as abstract thinking, writing, learning, and mathematical and language skills; and fantasizing; as well as making informed decisions. It is the habitat of our personality. The new brain tries to rationally explain our feelings, and the key role in it is played by the prefrontal cortex, unique to humans. There, not only the ability to plan actions, consider various alternatives and anticipate their positive and negative consequences, but also self-awareness are located. The new brain, involved in considering the long-term consequences of its own decisions, simultaneously tries to control impulsive reactions and selectively focus attention. It helps in avoiding purely habitual or instinctive behaviours and subordinates individual's activity to the goals set. By controlling the functioning of the emotional brain, the new brain suppresses emotional responses and ensures that the basis of an action is not only intuition and fleeting moods.

## Note

1 An interesting fact is that the amygdala is the brain structure that most thoroughly distinguishes the brain of women from the brain of men (Magrini 2017).

## Literature

Calne D., 2010, *Within Reason: Rationality and Human Behavior*, Vintage, New York.

Du Plessis E., 2011, *The Branded Mind, What Neuroscience Really Tells Us about the Puzzle of the Brain and the Brand*, Kogan Page, London.

Harari Y.N., 2015, *Sapiens – A Brief History of Humankind*, Harper Collins Publishers, New York.

Magrini M., 2017, *Cervello. Manuale dell'utente. Guida semplificata alla macchina più complessa del mundo*, Giunti Editore, Firenze-Milano.

Parry R., 2013, *Delivering the Neural Nudge*, MSQ Partners, London.
Pradeep A.K., 2010, *The Buying Brain: Secrets for Selling to the Subconscious Mind*, John Wiley and Sons, Hoboken, NJ.
Renvoisé P., Morin Ch., 2007, *Neuromarketing: Understanding the 'Buy Buttons' in Your Customer's Brain*, Thomas Nelson, Nashville.
Van Praet D., 2012, *Unconscious Branding: How Neuroscience Can Empower (And Inspire) Marketing*, Palgrave Macmillan, New York.
Waytz A., Mason M., 2013, Your Brain at Work, *Harvard Business Review*, July–August, pp. 103–111.

# APPENDIX 2

## Category penetration

Penetration can also be calculated for product categories.

**Metric definition**

*Category penetration* is the percentage of all consumers purchasing a product, at least once, over a specified period of time.

**Metric calculation**

Product category penetration rate
= 100 * number of buyers of the category,
even one-off : total number of consumers

Category penetration can be estimated on the basis of consumer surveys, consumer panels or a Target Group Index (TGI) survey. The penetration rates for selected product categories can also be calculated when we know the average consumption of the product in households registering its consumption, and among all households surveyed. Those data may be available in official statistics[1]:

Product category penetration rate
= 100 * average consumption of the product in households
registering its consumption : average consumption
in all households

The penetration rates for selected products are presented in Table A2.1.

The varied popularity of food products in different types of households is determined more by habits, different tastes or age-related gastric problems than disposable income. And what are the implications for brands?

**TABLE A2.1** Average monthly penetration of selected products in Poland (2018) by category of household

| | *Total* | *Self-employed* | *Non-manual labour* | *Manual labour* | *Retirees* | *Pensioners* | *Farmers* |
|---|---|---|---|---|---|---|---|
| Mineral and spring waters | **84.7** | 88.6 | 89.1 | 86.6 | 77.3 | 71.2 | 83.8 |
| Yogurt | **82.5** | 86.9 | 88.1 | 85.2 | 73.7 | 69.3 | 83.3 |
| Coffee | **78.3** | 71.4 | 71.4 | 81.0 | 72.7 | 73.5 | 84.2 |
| Fruit and vegetable juices | **68.3** | 77.3 | 76.2 | 72.2 | 51.6 | 48.4 | 64.8 |
| Fish and seafood | **59.6** | 62.8 | 61.0 | 56.4 | 60.6 | 52.2 | 60.9 |
| Breakfast cereals | **53.6** | 62.1 | 58.6 | 56.5 | 34.2 | 32.5 | 54.6 |

Source: Own calculations based on *Household Budgets 2018* (2019).

### Metric interpretation

The analysis of the category penetration rates can be very useful when defining the target audience for a given brand. Let's take one example. If breakfast cereals have almost double penetration among households of the self-employed and those working in non-manual labour positions than among households of retirees and pensioners, it can be safely assumed that in the buyer profile of the vast majority of breakfast cereal brands (especially those with large market shares), managers and entrepreneurs' households are over-represented, and retirees and pensioners' households are under-represented.

## Note

1 For example, in *Household Budgets*, published annually by the Polish Central Statistical Office.

## Literature

*Household Budgets 2018*, 2019, GUS, Warszawa: Glowny Urzad Statystyczny.

# APPENDIX 3

## Additional metrics regarding repeat and first-time buyers

Having information on the average number of packages of a brand[1] bought by an average customer in a given period of time, one can calculate many interesting metrics (Ehrenberg and Goodhardt 1978). Calculated using the formulas given below, the values almost perfectly reflect the numbers actually observed, as long as the brand operates in a stable market, consumers have considerable experience with the product and do not change their preferences under the influence of newly acquired information.

Let's say that we know that the average number of brand X packages bought in a year (*w*) is six.

The percentage of repeat buyers among all brand customers is calculated as

$$\text{Percentage of customers repeating brand purchase} = 2 \star (1 - w) : (1 - 2.3w) \quad \text{(A3.1)}$$

In this case, among all buyers of brand X in a given year, 78% are repeat purchasers and 22% are one-off buyers.

We can also calculate how much of the brand's sales come from buyers who repeat the purchase. The formula is a little bit more complicated now:

$$\text{Percentage of sales attributed torepeat buyers} = 1.23 \star (w - 1)^{1.23} : \left[1.23 \star (w - 1)^{1.23} + 0.5\right] \quad \text{(A3.2)}$$

It turns out that 94.7% of the brand's sales comes from repeat buyers, and only 5.3% from one-off customers.

Having the percentage of sales attributed to repeat brand buyers ($q$), we can calculate the average number of packages purchased by consumers buying a brand for the first time:

$$\text{Number of packages purchased by first-time brand buyers} = q : \ln\left(1+q\right) \tag{A3.3}$$

Thus, in our case, the average number of packages purchased by brand trialists is 1.42.

In turn, the number of packages purchased by repeat buyers of the brand is calculated as

$$\text{Number of packages purchased by repeat buyers of the brand} = -q^2 : \left[\left(1-q\right) \star \ln\left(1-q^2\right)\right] \tag{A3.4}$$

Buyers who repeated the purchase of brand X bought on average 7.4 packs in a year.

Certainly, the above metrics may impress participants during the presentation of a brand's health, especially in a situation where no additional expensive research was carried out to determine those metrics.

## Note

1 In order to calculate the value $w$ (average number of brand X packages purchased), it is enough to know the volume of sales of the brand and the number of its buyers, which can be obtained by multiplying the penetration rate by the total number of category buyers.

## Literature

Ehrenberg A.S.C., Goodhardt G.J., 1978, *The Anatomy of Buyer Behavior: Essays on Understanding Buyer Behavior*, J. Walter Thompson and Market Research Corporation of America, New York.

# APPENDIX 4

## Brand Development Index

A brand's market share (see Section 7.2) relates to the entire (in a geographical sense) market (the whole country). Meanwhile, an analysis of the geographical diversity of a brand's penetration in various product categories (possible, among others, thanks to the Target Group Index) shows a strong variation in brand popularity in different regions, which is usually much greater than between different consumer segments defined in demographic or socio-economic terms (excluding income or wealth). In other words, the same brand sells in different regions of a country with varying levels of success. In some regions, it might be caused by the presence of extremely strong local players, who effectively hamper the sales of a given brand. In many cases, it is quite obvious the region that a particular brand comes from, because its sales per capita there are usually higher than the average for the whole country.

The *Brand Development Index* (BDI) is calculated as

$$\text{Brand Development Index} = 100 \star \text{brand sales per capita in a given region} \left(\text{or market segment}\right) : \text{brand sales per capita across the country}$$

Only analyzing sales per capita, we can eliminate the influence of the population size of the region, and prove therefore the real market success of the brand if the BDI for the region is high.

The value of the BDI in individual regions/segments fluctuates around 100, informing the brand manager how much better/worse the brand sells in the region/segment, compared to the national average. So, if for region X its BDI is, say, 120, this means that the brand sells 20% better there, than the national average; if its BDI is e.g. 75, this means that in a given region sales per capita are 25% lower than the national average.

'Selling better/worse than the average...' does not necessarily mean that in a given region a brand sells more/less volume than in other regions, as it depends on the number of consumers in each region. A high BDI value does not necessarily mean that the brand is a sales leader in a given region. It may be generally a small brand that sells better than average in one of the regions, but still having an insignificant market share there. A high BDI value should also not be equated with a high level of brand penetration in the region (maybe the number of brand buyers is not large, but the brand has a large share of wallet), nor with a high level of customer loyalty (maybe the average buyer does not buy a given brand in large quantities, but there are many brand buyers). So what does the BDI tell us?

An analysis of the BDI in individual regions (segments) helps in determining whether the brand has a more or less equally strong position in the whole country (e.g. if its BDIs are 90, 95, 115, 100, 105) or quite the opposite: its position is very diverse (it would then have BDIs of 50, 60, 160, 140, 30). Maybe even the market success of the brand depends on its strong position in only one or two regions (BDIs of 10, 20, 300, 350, 5)?

**Case**

*In 2002, Actimel's (cultured yogurt by Danone) BDI in various regions of the UK varied from 131 in London and 123 in Central and North Scotland, to 74 in Yorkshire and 71 in Lancashire (Binet and Field 2007).*

Concentrating on selected regions (segments) has its advantages, because it allows the brand owner to focus usually limited marketing and sales resources on a few regions and not spread them thinly over the whole country. A too small scale of expenses, spread over many regions can make a brand invisible in the media, in the public sphere and in stores. What's more, a strong position in one or two regions, based on tested distribution and communication activities, can be a good starting point for expansion into other regions, when the intention is to conquer the entire country.

Yet, a strong regional brand that has built its position on perfectly matching the offer to very specific local tastes, may have problems with nationwide expansion (local taste might be a barrier to expansion to national retail chains). If a brand comes from a region with very specific tastes (e.g. culinary ones), then it may encounter difficulties in convincing customers from other parts of the country of its benefits and attributes.

The BDI is worth confronting with an analogous but product-related metric, the so-called Category Development Index (CDI), which is calculated as

$$\text{Category Development Index}$$
$$= 100 \star \text{product sales per capita in a given region}$$
$$\left(\text{or market segment}\right) : \text{product sales per capita across the country}$$

Its interpretation is identical to that of the BDI. CDI values above 100 indicate that the product sells better than average in the region; and below 100 that it sells worse than average in the country.

### Case

*Examples of CDI values for selected food products are presented in Table A4.1. It is worth noting here that even greater differences are registered in the case of products that do not meet basic needs (such as food).*

Of course, there is a fundamental difference between the BDI and the CDI: the variations in BDI scores are, in huge part, dependent on the scale of the resources engaged by the brand owner, and the effectiveness of their management. In the case of the CDI, the brand owner has no major impact on it, because a strong variation in product per capita consumption (e.g. the consumption of beetroot in Eastern Poland is two-thirds higher than the average for the country and 2.5 times higher than in Northern and North-west Poland) results mainly (in the case of food) from culinary traditions, local cuisine, local customs and preferences.

For the optimal apportionment of marketing and sales resources between regions, Figure A4.1 is useful as it simultaneously analyzes brand and category development indices.

The adoption of threshold values for the separation of regions with a high/low BDI and CDI will depend on the variation of those metrics for a given brand and category. Certainly, a BDI of 105 does not indicate that the brand sells exceptionally well in a region, and a CDI of 95 does lend support to suggestions that a product sells extremely poorly there. The cut-off points for both the BDI and the

**TABLE A4.1** Category Development Index for selected food products in Poland (2018 r.)

| *Products* | *Central* | *South* | *East* | *North-west* | *South-west* | *North* | *Mazovia (with capital city)* |
|---|---|---|---|---|---|---|---|
| Milk | 96.26 | 92.52 | 119.05 | 94.22 | 100.00 | 105.78 | 95.24 |
| Cream | 97.14 | 91.43 | 137.14 | 97.14 | 111.43 | 88.57 | 82.86 |
| Butter | 96.00 | 116.00 | 88.00 | 120.00 | 100.00 | 96.00 | 88.00 |
| Apples | 112.37 | 92.78 | 120.62 | 89.69 | 93.81 | 89.69 | 110.31 |
| Berries | 102.38 | 90.48 | 123.81 | 83.33 | 97.62 | 92.86 | 107.14 |
| Potatoes | 119.19 | 86.53 | 122.22 | 96.63 | 92.26 | 104.38 | 91.25 |
| Tomatoes | 123.46 | 86.42 | 103.70 | 91.36 | 98.77 | 98.77 | 114.81 |
| Cucumbers | 112.50 | 79.17 | 131.25 | 81.25 | 100.00 | 97.92 | 114.58 |
| Beetroots | 105.56 | 94.44 | 161.11 | 66.67 | 88.89 | 66.67 | 100.00 |
| Carrots | 109.09 | 97.73 | 129.55 | 81.82 | 100.00 | 93.18 | 97.73 |
| Sugar | 135.11 | 95.74 | 131.91 | 89.36 | 85.11 | 85.11 | 89.36 |
| Confectionery | 75.00 | 95.83 | 83.33 | 104.17 | 91.67 | 133.33 | 91.67 |
| Mineral and spring waters | 87.19 | 103.16 | 97.37 | 90.88 | 112.28 | 97.72 | 120.00 |
| Fruit and vegetable juices | 93.94 | 107.07 | 84.85 | 103.03 | 106.06 | 100.00 | 109.82 |

Source: Own calculations based on *Household Budgets 2018* (2019).

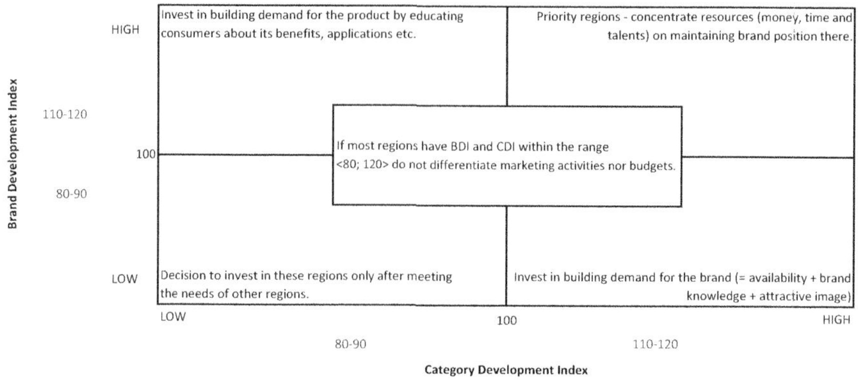


**FIGURE A4.1** Recommendations for regional marketing from BDI and CDI analysis.

**TABLE A4.2** BDI and CDI for a hypothetical brand of cream

| | *Central* | *South* | *East* | *North-west* | *South-west* | *North* | *Mazovia (with capital city)* |
|---|---|---|---|---|---|---|---|
| CDI (real values) | 97.14 | 91.43 | 137.14 | 97.14 | 111.43 | 88.57 | 82.86 |
| BDI (hypothetical values) | 100.00 | 90.00 | 65.00 | 85.00 | 80.00 | 145.00 | 175.00 |

CDI will be around 110–120 for 'high', and 80–90 for 'low'. In a situation where the BDI and the CDI for most regions are in the range <80–90, 110–120>, there are probably no reasons for differentiating the scale of involvement (marketing, sales) in individual regions, nor for different marketing strategies to be implemented there.

## Example

Returning to Figure A4.1, the owner of, say, a brand of cream has determined the BDI and the CDI for individual regions, obtaining values as in Table A4.2. It should be clearly stated that the distinct position of a brand and product in individual regions indicates the need for regional marketing.

Our hypothetical brand of cream probably comes from the Mazovia region, where it sells 75% better than the national average. The problem is that the sales of cream per capita there is 17% lower than the national average. A similar situation is in the Northern region: a brand sells almost 50% better there than the country's average, but cream sells 12% worse. In turn, in the Eastern region, where cream sells best (two-thirds better than in Mazovia), the brand's sales per capita are well below the national average (by one-third). In this situation, implementing exactly the same marketing activities in Mazovia and the Eastern region would not be effective. Activities in the East should focus on strengthening the brand's position there (after a more thorough analysis of the competitive situation in that region), and in Mazovia on increasing cream consumption which should be profitable for the brand, especially when it is a regional sales leader.

## Literature

Binet L., Field P., 2007, *Marketing in the Era of Accountability: Identifying the Marketing Practices and Metrics That Truly Increase Profitability*, World Advertising Research Center, Henley-on-Thames, p. 84.

*Household Budgets 2018*, 2019, GUS, Warszawa: Glowny Urzad Statystyczny.

# INDEX

Printed in Great Britain
by Amazon

59388350R00086